The Unbearable
Heaviness of Governing

The Unbearable Heaviness of Governing

The Obama Administration in Historical Perspective

Morton Keller

HOOVER INSTITUTION PRESS

STANFORD UNIVERSITY | STANFORD, CALIFORNIA

The Hoover Institution on War, Revolution and Peace, founded at Stanford University in 1919 by Herbert Hoover, who went on to become the thirty-first president of the United States, is an interdisciplinary research center for advanced study on domestic and international affairs. The views expressed in its publications are entirely those of the authors and do not necessarily reflect the views of the staff, officers, or Board of Overseers of the Hoover Institution.

www.hoover.org

Hoover Institution Press Publication No. 601

Hoover Institution at Leland Stanford Junior University, Stanford, California, 94305–6010

First printing 2010
16   15   14   13   12   11   10   7   6   5   4   3   2   1

Manufactured in the United States of America

The paper used in this publication meets the minimum Requirements of the American National Standard for Information Sciences—Permanence of Paper for Printed Library Materials, ANSI/NISO Z39.48–1992. ∞

Cataloging-in-Publication Data is available from Library of Congress
ISBN-13: 978–0–8179–1264–2 (cloth. : alk. paper)
ISBN-13: 978–0–8179–1266–6 (e-book)

To the Republic, a quarter of a millennium young

CONTENTS

FOREWORD

THE HOOVER INSTITUTION has embarked on a working group to assess some of the critical junctures we have experienced in American government and politics, which seem to have evoked dramatic changes set in motion by the 2008 election. The objective is to call on political scientists and historians to address the unfolding policy agendas of government, the politics of policy, and the growth of the administrative state. *The Unbearable Heaviness of Governing: The Obama Presidency in Historical Perspective* is the first endeavor to emerge from the group's efforts.

The current membership of the working group includes David Brady, Morris P. Fiorina, Morton Keller, and James Q. Wilson. Future efforts of the group are forthcoming.

John Raisian
Tad and Dianne Taube Director,
Hoover Institution, Stanford University

ACKNOWLEDGMENTS

MY THANKS go to colleagues and/or friends for helpful counsel, encouragement, and correction: Dave Brady, Moe Fiorina, Jim Wilson, Ken Shepsle, and Pietro Nivola, fellow-participants in the Hoover Institution's Working Group on Critical Junctures in American Government and Politics; Stephan and Abigail Thernstrom and Marc Landy; Hoover Director John Raisian; the wonderfully efficient staff of the Hoover Institution Press; and (as always) my wife Phyllis.

Introduction

D URING HIS Harvard student days, humorist Robert Benchley, in a hung-over state, confronted a diplomatic history exam. It asked him to discuss the Newfoundland fisheries dispute. "This topic has been exhaustively examined from the viewpoint of the United States, Great Britain, and Canada," he began. "I shall discuss it from the viewpoint of the fish."

Now that we are well and truly into the Obama years, it is time for a progress report that rests less on the day-to-day perspective of most pundits and politicians and more on the longer (if often tunnel-visioned) perspective of history: that sea of time and change in which we citizen-fish swim.

In the course of writing this book, I came to realize that I was confronted by a dilemma, encountered by every president, that is the precise antithesis of the one explored by Milan Kundera in his great novel *The Unbearable Lightness of Being*. Kundera's protagonists struggle with the inescapable reality that their private life—their being—is self-contained, brief, isolated, purposeless: in short, "light." (Kundera: "I have no mission. No one has.")

But as president, Barack Obama carries a very different weight. It might be called an "unbearable heaviness" in the sense that whatever his talents or aspirations—and surely a sense of mission is the essence of his presidency—Obama is constrained by the past, by his institutional surround, and by the course of events.

Hence *The Unbearable Heaviness of Governing*: Obama's burden, but hardly his alone.[1]

Comparing our presidents with their predecessors is one way to grasp more fully the character and quality of their performances. This has been notably so in the case of Barack Obama, because of the special aura of his persona, his talents, and his ambition.

In his meteoric career, Obama has been linked to a number of history's great men. References to Jesus Christ, God, and Abraham Lincoln flowed from the pens of irrationally exuberant disciples and journalists. National Endowment for the Arts chairman Rocco Landesman thought that as a memoirist Obama was "the most powerful writer since Julius Caesar." A premature Nobel Peace Prize, and journalist Jacob Weisberg's prediction that if he secured Obamacare by the time of his first State of the Union address he will have "accomplished more in his first year than any other postwar American president," were other triumphs of illusion over reality. The two most conspicuous books on Obama so far, David Remnick's *The Bridge* and Jonathan Alter's *The Promise*, bear titles with a messianic resonance.[2]

But this mid-term report does not confine itself to the parlor game of presidential analogy. It examines as well the larger realities that are shaping Obama's presidency: the facts of contemporary political life; the nature of key institutions such as Congress and the bureaucracy; and that all-too-frequent determiner of a president's destiny, the course of events.

The focus here is more on the context in which Obama is making his way than on his talents and intentions. The latter are what he brought to the great game of government; the former determine the rules of the game.

▪ ▪ ▪

In the first flush of the Obama incumbency, the analogue of FDR's Hundred Days assumed a large place in the media. Those standard-bearers the *New York Times* and the *Washington Post* linked "Obama" and "100 Days" almost 900 times in the first six months of 2009.

And indeed the new administration's response to the financial crisis of late 2008 and early 2009 had a striking resonance with the even more fraught period of Franklin Delano Roosevelt's election in November 1932 and his early days in office in March 1933. The winter of 2008–2009, like the winter of 1932–1933, was dominated by dire news of unemployment (741,000 jobs lost in January 2009 alone), home forfeitures, and plummeting stocks.

Obama came into office in that dispiriting time on a wave of hope and expectation, much as FDR did in

March 1933. His response to the economic crisis was at first widely supported, as were FDR's early actions. His appointees were full of New Dealish get-up-and-go. He emulated his great predecessor by unleashing a flurry of large legislative initiatives: the economic stimulus package, health care reform, and a cap-and-trade energy bill to begin with; financial reform to follow; education and immigration reform down the road.

True, at the end of his talismanic Hundred Days, Obama's approval rating had dropped from its initial 70-plus percent to just over 60 percent. But this still was strong compared to Bill Clinton's and George W. Bush's 56 percent at comparable stages in their presidencies.

Then the story takes another turn. After the first victories—the Stimulus Act passed, the energy bill moved through the House—things slowed. The Democrats had solid majorities of about eighty votes in the House and close to a cloture-guaranteeing twenty in the Senate. And history taught that when the issue was large, and the party in power was well-ensconced, a number of opposition members could be induced to lend their support. Yet the stimulus bill won almost no GOP backers. Health care reform wound up solely supported by Democrats, and was opposed by almost half of that party's House majority.

This was at most New Deal/Great Society Lite: not a Hundred Days-like burst of innovative policymaking and administrative action, but a harsh grind of legislative gridlock and bureaucratic sclerosis, of the sort that has become common in modern American political life.

What are the conditions of the public culture that explain this course of events? Was it the nature of the issues, the character of modern American politics, the partisanship of the Democratic leaders, the obduracy of the Republicans?

We can start with the core concept of a presidency devoted to a large, integrated program. For a century, since Theodore Roosevelt's Square Deal and Woodrow Wilson's New Freedom, the lure of a programmatic presidency persisted, especially among Democratic chief executives steeped in an activist tradition. That programmatic impulse flowered with FDR's New Deal and Lyndon B. Johnson's Great Society.

The rise of post-1960s skepticism toward grand plans and the active state made the programmatic presidency ever more . . . yesterday. Still, the mantra persisted. Jimmy Carter spoke of a "New Foundation" in his 1977 State of the Union address. And Clinton launched the theme of a "New Covenant" in January 1995, airily designed to foster "opportunity, responsibility, and community."

Obama predictably adhered to the tradition in his 2009 Inaugural Address. Then, and more fully in a Georgetown University speech on April 14, 2009, he spoke of "A New Foundation for America." For a time, almost every public statement from the administration cited that label. But like other recent examples of the genre, the New Foundation hasn't taken hold. Through 2009 and the first half of 2010, the *Times* and the *Post* referred to it a not-so-grand total of forty-seven times.[3]

The greater autonomy of Congress and interest groups, along with general skepticism toward big government, work against the programmatic presidency. This is an age of strongly held beliefs rather than broadly defined ideologies. Separate pieces of legislation, with little of a larger context, do best: Clinton's NAFTA and welfare reform, Bush's tax cuts and No Child Left Behind.

Another feature of Obama's style of governance that sets him apart from FDR and LBJ is his reliance on congressional leaders for crafting his bills as well as shepherding their passage. Just as the New Deal and the Great Society, for all their fuzziness, had a defining character, so were FDR and LBJ markedly more controlling than Obama.

This is as much a product of Obama's political time as of his leadership style. The limited experience in governing that he shared with his closest advisers made him all the less likely to assert himself against the self-reliant congressional barons or his advocacy group supporters.

That has saved him so far from an adversarial relationship with his party's congressional leadership of the sort endured by Carter. An autonomous, non-dependent congressional leadership, a president with little taste for the grubby business of lawmaking, and a core of parochial advisers are representative products of contemporary political culture.

Finally, it is not at all clear that the times are out of joint in precisely the way that Obama imagines they are.

The sense (and the reality) of systemic economic failure that swept over America in the Great Depression, or the social-cultural malaise generated in the 1960s by the civil rights movement, Vietnam, and the counterculture, have no real analogues today.

True, joblessness is joblessness, and alienation is alienation. But scale does make a difference. And it can be argued that what most ails America today is not as readily subject to legislative nostrums as was the case in the 1930s and the 1960s. Indeed, large numbers of Americans think that more government is the problem, not the solution.

The distinctive character of the present time and context has left its mark on the policy and politics of the early Obama years. There is no sign of a swelling tide of political response to Obama's policies or indeed his presidency of the sort that so altered, while it solidly enlarged, the Democratic predominance of the 1930s. The persistence of much popular unhappiness with Obama's policies and—so far—marginally more content than discontent with him as president, are indications that the identification of a chief executive with his program no longer has the defining power that it once had.

Making sense of this new world of politics and government is not easy. George Bush and Karl Rove misread their 2002 and 2004 election victories to signify that they were on the cusp of a normal Republican majority, repeating Newt Gingrich's mistake after the 1994 election. Obama and his advisers appeared to read into the 2006 and 2008 election returns a similar mandate for the Democrats. And as Bush-Rove moved away from reaching out across party lines, so has Obama set aside the campaign rhetoric of post-partisanship. He turned over the key components of his program—the stimulus package and health care reform—to a Democratic congressional leadership whose interest in cross-aisle comity was vanishingly small. Their Republican counterparts fully shared that sentiment.

Of course, this is only the first stage of a political journey which has between two and six years to go. What follows is a history-focused examination of Obama's developing style of governing and his signature policies: the stimulus and financial reform acts and Obamacare. We will then turn to what may lie ahead in the policy and political prospects of this fascinating chief executive, so subject to—and constrained by—the historical, institutional, and events-driven weight of American politics and government.

Governing

RAHM EMANUEL is reported to have said to President Obama at the end of 2009: "You know, Mr. President, Franklin Roosevelt had eight years to deal with the economy before he had to lead a war. You have to do it all at once."[1]

It's an old courtier's rule that you can't over-flatter the king. But this instance suffers from historical distortion. The Great Recession of 2008–2009 was not the Great Depression of 1929–1939. Nor are the Iraq Drawdown and the Afghan Surge the Second World War.

Still, it is easy to see why Obama's chief of staff adopted this mode of discourse. Comparisons (celebratory, derogatory, and analytical) of Obama with his heavyweight predecessor FDR were thick on the media ground before and during his accession to the presidency. But by the summer of 2009 it was widely noted that the fall in Obama's favorability rating, from the high 70s to the neighborhood of 50 percent, was the most substantial in the history of the modern presidency, with the exception of Gerald Ford.[2]

THE FIRST YEAR

Surely much of the explanation for this slide from grace lay in the fact that no chief executive could live up to expectations as elevated as those of his more ardent supporters (and, indeed, of himself). Nor is it surprising that the incumbent—even one so verbally gifted and attractive in public personality—would pay a price for unemployment that remained stubbornly high and a world scene that did not get noticeably more benign.

As the months passed, and the chattering classes endlessly parsed, it became common currency that both the style and substance of his governance had serious inadequacies. "Yes He Can," *Newsweek* tartly observed in November 2009, "(But He Sure Hasn't Yet)". Triumphal evocations of the New Deal and the Great Society faded. Hopeful analogies with a triangulating Bill Clinton, who survived into a second term, and more pessimistic ones with a star-plagued Jimmy Carter, who did not, became the norm.[3]

■ ■ ■

Obama hit the ground running in January 2009 with the élan expected by those who saw great things in him. His Inaugural Address did not quite match Lincoln's

Second (or even Lincoln's First). But it was an acceptably eloquent declaration of his intentions and beliefs. While he did not equal the early legislative outpourings of FDR and LBJ, his economic stimulus and budget bills were proposed and enacted with considerable dispatch. And major health care and energy legislation, core elements of his campaign platform, quickly came before Congress. Education and immigration waited expectantly in the wings.

In sum, an expeditious start for the New Foundation. But well within the Hundred Days that had come to serve as the gold standard for presidential leadership, doubts and reservations began to surface. Unlike Bush's TARP bank bailout, whose support (and opposition) were impressively bipartisan, Obama's stimulus package won the votes of no House and only three Senate Republicans. His budget fared no better.

Budgets are intensely partisan creations, and sharp party division is the norm. But the Stimulus Act was widely regarded as an extension of Bush's TARP: the next phase of a national, and not just a partisan, response to the biggest economic challenge since the Great Depression. Yet Obama sought neither to set the terms of this legislation nor to assure it a bipartisan face. Instead, he turned it over to the House leadership, who had no mantle of bipartisanship to discard. The result was in effect the requisition sheet of a Democratic-liberal wish list. The tropistic Republican impulse to oppose was amply nourished by this sustenance, and the result was the first partisan fire bell in the political night.

■ ■ ■

By the end of March, two months into Obama's term, *The Economist* summed up the prevailing view of the president: "Coming Down to Earth." By January 2010 the magazine (prematurely) found Obama's journey concluded: "The man who fell to earth." Mega-investor Warren Buffett, another supporter, worried that "you can't expect people to unite behind you if you're trying to jam a whole bunch of things down their throat."[4]

But Obama's ambitious legislative program was not in itself the problem. After all, he had given ample notice that his would be an active presidency. Rather, it appears to have been the disconnect between his campaign mantra of governing in a less partisan manner and transcending the old ways of the past, and the all-too-evident persistence of party politics, earmarks, lobbyists, and favored interests, that soured so much opinion so quickly.

That Obama sought to govern more from the Left than the center should have come as no surprise, given his political past and the leanings of his core supporters. But many of those who voted for him were not so ideologically inclined. While the Obama honeymoon was still under way, polls suggested that Americans if anything tended increasingly to lean conservative, not liberal. And the opinion infrastructure of the Right—Fox News, the *Wall Street Journal*, conservative bloggers, pundits, and think tanks—kept up a constant, and consequential, critical refrain.[5]

By the summer of 2009, Obama seemed to be losing his way. This was not unique: FDR went through several slack periods during the creation of the New Deal. The need to recalibrate is an accepted part of the presidential-legislative process. And Obama's congressional majorities, while solid, were less than those of FDR and LBJ (though certainly more than those of George W. Bush).[6]

The initially well-disposed Left found growing grounds for dissatisfaction, as both the substance and the implementation of its most valued legislative goals faltered. Obama's propensity for talk-fest "summits," though hardly his invention, came in for a pasting. More severe critics focused on what they took to be his underlying intentions. There was talk in the Right of his being the most left-wing president ever, of nurturing a socialist or at least a European social democratic agenda.[7]

▪ ▪ ▪

As comparisons with FDR and LBJ declined, analogies with Jimmy Carter grew. Columnist Peggy Noonan thought that, like Carter, Obama "was brilliant at becoming president but not being president." The other newly popular analogy, favored by those more predisposed to the president, was with Bill Clinton. Moderate Democratic consultant Douglas Schoen spoke hopefully of Obama emulating Clinton in tacking to the center. He remembered Clinton telling him: "I'm way out of position. I was elected as a centrist, and now I'm perceived as a liberal Dem[ocrat]. I have to change that, and I've got to put some space between myself and Congress."[8]

But Clinton himself, as seemed to be the case with Obama, initially read his victory as a mandate to respond to his party's ideological core rather than to the less committed center. Bush adviser Karl Rove observed that "Obama has not governed as the centrist, deficit-fighting, bipartisan consensus builder he promised to be. And his promise to embody a new kind of politics—free of finger-pointing, pettiness, and spin—was a mirage." Fair enough. But much the same could be said of the president Rove served—and of the counsel he offered.[9]

It is true that Bush got major legislation—substantial tax cuts, No Child Left Behind, the Patriot Act, Medicaid prescription coverage—through less favorable congressional terrain than Obama traverses. But he assumed an increasingly polarizing persona—political, ideological—that eventually earned him a national unpopularity well beyond anything that Obama has had to face.

This suggests that what led Obama to a strongly partisan course of leadership was not solely the dictates of ideology or the goad of high ambition, but a persisting reality in recent American politics. Polls show a strong predilection among the increasingly decisive independent voters for less intense partisanship, an ideological Middle Way. But the political class tends to favor the ideologically skewed and intensely partisan stances that their party cores prefer. Republican strategist Alex Castellanos observed: "Obama has tried so hard not to be George Bush and [the early] Bill Clinton, and yet he is becoming exactly that."[10]

Doubts about where Obama sought to lead the country merged with doubts as to the efficacy of his leadership style. The impression grew that he was drawing down on his stock of public goodwill by the frequency of his exposure and the repetitiveness of his public persona: mildly hectoring, more than a little professorial. Peggy Noonan observed: "He never seems to be leveling, only talking."

His reliance on a teleprompter became a source of ridicule. The satirical magazine *The Onion* reported a crisis in the Obama household: a teleprompter failure while he was lecturing one of his daughters during the family's Sunday dinner. Satire morphed into reality when two months later it emerged that Obama had used the device in a talk to elementary school children.[11]

Obama's reiterated commitment to systemic, foundational change and his readiness to let Congress tend to the legislative nuts and bolts while he devoted himself to didactic instruction of the masses is reminiscent of Carter. Even more, it summons up the shade of Woodrow Wilson. Like Wilson, Obama is most comfortable in an instructive mode. He gave 263 speeches in the first 233 days of his presidency, including 122 on health care reform—whose difficulties he blamed in part on his failure to sufficiently convey the bill's virtues. FDR gave only four fireside chats in 1933 and twenty-seven over the course of his twelve years in office.

Obama shied away from give-and-take with reporters, as media obeisance began to fade. From July 2009 to well into 2010, he held no formal press conferences.

FDR had almost a thousand of them in his long presidency.[12]

By early 2010 it appeared that the efficacy of the Obama leadership style was wearing a bit thin. His less-than-successful Olympics and global warming visits to Copenhagen, and most of all the frustrations attendant on his health care initiative, led the White House in February to announce a revamping of its communications strategy: to respond more quickly to his political opponents, to focus more intensely on his call for "change," to use his time more effectively. But changes in message or personnel were conspicuously absent; Obama displayed a Wilsonian stubbornness. Finally, in the March 2010 health care victory, his governing style—summed up by *New York Times* columnist David Brooks as half Harvard Economics department, half Boss Daley—chalked up a major success.[13]

PRESIDENT AND CONGRESS

An early analysis of Obama's prospects warned: "[he] must avoid forms of administrative aggrandizement that alienate citizens from government, and . . . must forego leadership strategies that threaten the independence and integrity of the party apparatus."[14] On the first count, his record so far has been decidedly mixed. On the second, it has been decidedly successful.

The most conspicuous measure for evaluating Obama's leadership is his success in getting Congress to enact his legislative program. Even when one party controls both branches, this is by no means inevitable. The message taught by history is clear. While the Democrats had substantial majorities of about eighty in the House and up to twenty in the Senate, the record of the past suggests that party predominance is a thin reed on which to rest the success of his program.

True, the threat of a presidential veto is not in play. But the constraint of a Senate filibuster, a device increasingly resorted to by both parties in recent years, made the sixty-vote requirement to invoke cloture an equally important check on simple majority rule. And it is a self-evident fact that the larger the Democratic majority, the more it includes members from often Republican-leaning states and districts, and hence the larger the number needed to avoid gridlock on a given piece of legislation.[15]

So far there is little evidence of the strains between president and Congress that so quickly characterized, and for so long plagued, the Carter administration. The members of the leadership could not but be pleased by Obama's readiness to let them take the legislative reins. Given the forces that feed the autonomy of members of Congress, Obama's readiness to do so may have been as necessary for him as it was satisfying to them.

But necessity did not foreclose difficulty. The left wing of the Democratic Party has as outsized a voice in Congress as Southern Democrats did in the pre-civil rights years. House Speaker Nancy Pelosi, Energy and Commerce chair Henry Waxman, Ways and Means chair (until March 2010) Charles Rangel, and Financial

Services chair Barney Frank represent constituencies as solidly Democratic, and as strongly Left-leaning (San Francisco affluent, black, Jewish), as the districts of the old Southern barons were bastions of white supremacist-Democratic sentiment. Of the twenty-one most influential House Democratic leaders, sixteen came from districts that went for Obama by an average of over 70 percent.[16]

Heavily blue-state California assumed the same dominance in the leadership that Texas had in the Rayburn-Johnson era, or the South at large before the 1960s. Pelosi symbolically defeated Texas Congressman Martin Frost to become Speaker. She saw to it that her fellow-liberal Californian Henry Waxman replaced the more accommodating John Dingell of Michigan as Energy and Commerce chair.

Other Californians in places of power were George Miller in Education and Labor, Jane Harman in Intelligence, and Senators Barbara Boxer in Environment and Public Works and Dianne Feinstein in Intelligence. When ethics problems forced Rangel to leave the chairmanship of Ways and Means, Pelosi initially sought to replace him with Pete Stark, yet another Californian, noted even in that free-wheeling political world for his off-the-charts remarks and behavior. This was a bit too provocative; he was quickly replaced by Sander Levin, a Michigan representative more closely attuned to mainstream America.[17]

On the eve of Obama's inauguration in December 2008, *The Economist* took note of the filibuster danger in the Senate, where the Democrats at the time were one shy of the sixty seats needed to invoke cloture. The journal thought that this would induce Obama to refrain from narrowly partisan lawmaking and restore the tradition of bipartisan votes on major legislation. It estimated that there were about twenty-three centrist Republican and Democratic senators; it was to them that Obama should turn.[18]

Why did Obama instead give over his legislative agenda to the highly polarized leadership of Congress? Just as Democratic presidents from FDR to LBJ had to deal with the at-times politically dysfunctional consequences of the Southern leaders, so it might have seemed prudent to rein in the Californians. It would be difficult to argue that Pelosi, Waxman, and Company embodied mainstream American political attitudes.

There has not been much evidence (or at least reportage) of tension, ideological or procedural, between Obama and the congressional leadership. Journalist Matt Bai observed that Obama's is "the most Congress-centric administration in modern history." Presumably not unrelated is the fact that Obama has issued fewer executive orders than his immediate predecessors: less than fifty by the end of March 2010. FDR produced 674 in his first fifteen months, LBJ 130 in 1964 and 1965.[19]

Explanations for this deference abound. Surely one has to do with Obama's clear preference for the art of public persuasion over the craft of bill-making. He seems most at ease facing a supportive audience, a photogenic human backdrop behind him, teleprompters purring. Only when health care entered into its climactic gridlock phase did he throw himself into the legislative mosh pit.[20]

The disparity between the promise of a Hundred Days or a Great Society, and the reality of an increasingly frustrating year-plus culminating in the drawn-out health care imbroglio, cast a shadow over Obama's dealings with Congress and his legislative agenda. There are structural (or, in the jargon of our time, systemic) reasons for the character of that relationship. The increased autonomy of senators and representatives, with their own funding, single-minded constituencies, and decreasing reliance on their party or their leadership, is a prime fact of modern American political life.[21]

For all that, Obama's initial record of accomplishment was by no means picayune. The stimulus package, a $3.6 trillion budget, the energy and health care bills passed by the House, expanded health care for children and an increase in the minimum wage, a broad reform of the financial system: these were respectable accomplishments. And in March 2010 the administration staggered, shakily but triumphantly, over the finish line in the race to enact Obamacare.

RUNNING THE PRESIDENCY

How much experience in governing did Obama have before he became president? In the words of the senior civil servant in BBC's *Yes Minister*, when asked how many women were in senior posts in his ministry: "Approximately none." His lack of exposure to either running an organization or (save for a stint in the Illinois state senate and a truncated U.S. Senate term) holding public office sets him apart from almost all his modern predecessors, Democratic or Republican.

FDR, Reagan, Clinton, Carter, and Bush II governed states: all but Clinton, major ones. Truman, LBJ, and Ford were consequential senators or Congressmen; JFK bolstered an extended, if lackluster, congressional record with his war hero status. Eisenhower led and won the war against Hitler; Bush I held a rich variety of high government posts. Obama's lean political background was matched only by Carter's and Woodrow Wilson's two-year/one-term governorships.

Like Carter and Wilson, Obama capitalized on his above-everyday-politics persona and scant political record to win election to the presidency. As Carter painfully discovered, the qualities that made him so effective a candidate did not readily transfer to the nuts and bolts of governance. Election is an event, specific and time-confined. Governing is a condition, amorphous and indeterminate.

How has Obama gone about running his slice of the modern American presidency? During the campaign there was a tension between his emphasis on a post-partisan, ameliorating politics and his previous political persona. That included a dab of Chicago Saul Alinsky-style community organizing, close links to a radical black pastor and ties with onetime terrorist William

Ayers, and by one measure the Senate's most liberal voting record. Yet while Obama was harsh on his predecessor in his Inaugural Address and subsequent comments, his dominant campaign tone was outreach and reconciliation.

Obama's initial actions generally reflected that more moderate mode. The appointments of Timothy Geithner as secretary of the treasury and Lawrence Summers as his chief economic adviser were hardly sops to the Left. Nicolas Sarkozy-like, he looted the opposition by keeping Bush's Secretary of Defense Robert Gates and Federal Reserve chief Ben Bernanke. He offered the job of secretary of commerce to Republican New Hampshire Senator Judd Gregg (who accepted and then changed his mind); he made GOP Congressmen John McHugh secretary of the army, Ray LaHood secretary of transportation, and ex-Congressman Jim Leach head of the National Endowment for the Humanities.[22]

Glitches common to new administrations did appear: enough of them for *The Economist* to observe that the big surprise in his first two months was "a certain lack of competence." His attempt to make former Senate Majority Leader Tom Daschle his health care czar ran aground on ethics issues; Treasury Secretary Geithner had to overcome a bad patch over tax problems.[23]

■ ■ ■

Is there a larger pattern, or character, to the emergent Obama administration? FDR's New Deal was shaped by a flow of new people—Jews, Catholics, academics, social workers—into realms of policymaking that (except during World War I) previously had been closed to them. Harry Truman drew on a World War II-nurtured group of "wise men" to respond to the challenge of the cold war. John F. Kennedy relied on "action intellectuals" (Robert McNamara, McGeorge Bundy, Walt Rostow, Dean Rusk). Lyndon Johnson used all the above, as well as his own unique powers of persuasion and intimidation.[24]

And Obama? It is not clear who his equivalent wise men are aside from the Summers-Geithner-Peter Orszag economic team; or, indeed, *if* they are. So far, the most influential advisers appear to be his "Chicago Mafia": longtime associates who came with him. The most obvious analogy is with Jimmy Carter's "Georgia Mafia."

That tightly knit group consists of Chief of Staff Rahm Emanuel (Obama's Hamilton Jordan—and perhaps his Dick Cheney?), political adviser David Axelrod (Obama's Bert Lance—and perhaps his Karl Rove?), senior adviser Valerie Jarrett (comparable to Rosalynn Carter?), and (the lone outsider) press secretary Robert Gibbs (his Jody Powell?).

Just as Carter remained close to his white, Protestant, small town/rural fellow-Georgians, so does Obama's inner circle—two Jews, one African American, and the (somewhat less close) southerner Gibbs—satisfy the evident psychological needs of a president who, like Carter, does not make friends easily and came with a relative outsider's relationship to the world of high politics in Washington. Obama's Chicago "Politburo," like Carter's Georgia or Clinton's Arkansas (or Nixon's California) group of intimates, has had to surmount the stigmas of parochialism and inexperience, and so far has done at least as well as their predecessors.[25]

One difference: Powell, Jordan, and Lance, and indeed Carter himself, were less committed to an ideologically defined agenda than seems to be the case with the Obama inner circle—excepting Emanuel, who is supposed to be more disposed to making compromises and cutting deals than the others.

The chief of staff is normally the point man in White House governance. This is especially so in Emanuel's case because of his take-no-prisoners personality and, more importantly, his role as the administration's chief contact man with a Congress whose leadership is in charge of much of the Obama program. Emanuel's assertiveness might be expected to foster bureaucratic food fights over primacy of place. He is said to have boasted early on that his West Wing office was eight square feet larger than the vice president's; his Rolodex was reported to sag under the weight of six thousand names.[26]

But there is no sign that the president wants a first among equals on his staff: a counterpart, say, to Wilson's Colonel House or FDR's Harry Hopkins or George Bush's Karl Rove. The customarily unflappable Obama was reported to have erupted in anger when a *New York Times Magazine* profile of Valerie Jarrett spoke of tension between her and Emanuel. Then came a *Washington Post* story touting Emanuel as the voice of moderation on the staff, counseling against the failed Copenhagen-Olympics trip and calling for a more restrained health care bill. As in most administrations, the chief of staff becomes a focal point for evaluations of how the president is managing things. Supporters dwell on his indispensability; critics on how he is leading his boss astray.[27]

▪ ▪ ▪

It is still premature to characterize the Obama bureaucracy. In part this is because it has been slow to emerge, a recurring feature of modern administrations; in part because the media—more focused on Obama the president and issues such as health care than on the actual workings of government—have paid relatively little attention to the subject. (This may reflect as well a general decline of interest in institutions and how they work. Since Obama came into office, there has been a dearth of reportage on power brokers and lobbyists—not, one assumes, because these have disappeared from the Washington scene.)[28]

Critics on the Right have fastened on intermittent flaps over second-level or lesser appointees, such as Van Jones, who are sufficiently far left to topple over into unacceptability. This is not unlike the drip of revelations of over-the-top conservative appointees during the Bush years. Both are the inevitable accompaniments of administrations with a strong ideological bent.[29]

More noticeable is the increase in appointees who are black or female (or both), went to Ivy League schools, and are *not* Christian, Southern, or business men or women. This was to be expected of the party change in 2008. As of June 2009, only nine of Obama's twenty-two Cabinet choices, and fewer than half of his 366 top executive branch appointments, were white men.

But the changes were not dramatic. Men made up 74 percent of Bush's appointees and 66 percent of Obama's. White Christians constituted 71 percent of Bush's appointees; 65 percent of Obama's. Total black appointments were 11 percent under Bush, the same as under Obama; Bush did minutely better than Obama on Hispanics and Asians.

There has been no conspicuous New Dealer-like influx of idealistic young people to give a distinctive tone to the Obama administration. Part of the reason may be the very different recruitment ground today, as compared to the early 1930s. Now there is an infrastructure of think tanks, foundations, and university research centers, ready to provide cadres of experts who are far from short in the tooth. And the demands of governance are so much more complex today that Obama has been understandably loath to bypass these recruiting grounds.[30]

■ ■ ■

The aspect of the Obama bureaucracy that initially drew the greatest attention—for the most part critical—was the influx of "czars." Appointees unvetted by Congress appeared in World Wars I and II; Nixon appointed

William Simon as energy czar in the 1970s. The difference now is of scale. By bypassing the hazardous path of congressional review, these appointees may be a counterweight to the administration's inclination to defer to the legislature on policymaking. More than twenty of Obama's early appointees were elevated to czardom. Their remits included the economy (Lawrence Summers), health care (Nancy-Ann DeParle), energy (the EPA's Carol Browner), violence against women, drugs, securing our borders, urban matters, stimulus accountability, Iran, the Middle East, the auto industry, business regulation, and cyber-security. A peak of sorts was the summer 2010 recess appointment of Dr. Donald Berwick to head the Centers for Medicare & Medicaid Services, thus dodging potentially radioactive congressional hearings on the appointee's views on socialized medicine and health care rationing.

Conservatives predictably saw in this Big Government running amok; liberals predictably were undisturbed by worthily non-Republican public servants. The somewhat odorous Van Jones, special adviser for green jobs, enterprise, and innovation, was an embarrassment; executive compensation czar Kenneth Feinberg is widely praised for doing the Lord's work.

In a number of cases these were add-ons to areas that already were somebody's (or several somebodies') turf, such as energy and the Middle East. Jurisdictional disputes seemed inevitable. But, again, the media have not been much interested in this realm of Your Tax Dollars at Work.[31]

The growth of czars may properly be seen as an adaptation to a bureaucracy that belongs to the culture of the modern American state, more than to the change in party rule. Government at all levels—national, state, and local—employs some 23 million people. Eighteen percent of them work for the federal government; if one subtracts the Postal Service and the military, the portion is 10 percent. Employment in Washington—the belly of the bureaucratic beast—is only about 150,000, and has been at that level since the early 1970s (though there has been a recent uptick).

The lower levels of government employment have grown steadily more attractive, the result of strong unions, more-than-competitive salaries, job security, and husky health care and pension benefits. But there has been a long-term decline in the relative attractiveness of upper civil service positions. Salaries are significantly less than those in comparable private sector work. The hiring process has become more onerous and intrusive. Responsibility, accountability, and the ability to make and enforce decisions are subject to an ever more cumbersome, multi-layered bureaucracy.

This combination of a government workforce minimally subject to competitive spurs to high performance, and a bureaucratic elite maximally subject to the superior attractions of the private sector, does not bode well for the high ambitions of the Obama administration. Its goals require the greatly increased recruitment of managerial-professional regulators. To attract able people will require compensation and perks that may foster competitive tensions with the blue-collar public service unions. But it is clear that the Democratic hiring pool includes far more people attracted by government work than does its GOP counterpart.[32]

THE ABUSE OF POWER

A recurring theme in modern American government is the relationship between the increased power of the state and the threat this poses to the rights and freedoms of individuals. In the past that concern has been associated with the deprivation of civil liberties in wartime. Lincoln, Wilson, FDR, and LBJ faced substantial criticism on this ground: the more divided was opinion on the war, the fiercer the reaction.

The Bush administration's record on the treatment of detainees accused of terrorism—charges of torture or rendition to less constrained governments, detention at Guantanamo, the improper use of wiretaps to obtain intelligence, unconstitutional constraints on the disposition of cases—had a prominent place in the media and in Democratic criticism before and during the campaign.

To what degree has the Obama administration embarked on a new course of openness, lawfulness, and restraint? Guantanamo, and most of the methods used by the Bush administration (wiretaps, rendition, etc.), are still with us, and are likely to remain so. Civil liberties groups have been disappointed early and often with the Obama record. Attorney General Eric Holder's preference for civilian over military trials ran into serious problems with the Detroit would-be airplane bomber and the disposition of 9/11 conspirator Khalid Sheikh Mohammed. But whether this was a measure of the faults of the administration or the unrealistic expectations of its critics, remains an open question.[33]

However strong the commitment to openness, the dictates of governing inevitably put a premium on secrecy. Thus it was no easy task to secure data as to precisely which cars (gas-savers or gas-guzzlers? domestic or foreign?) consumers were in fact buying under the Cash for Clunkers program in the summer of 2009. Lobbyists were to be excluded from the corridors of power. But there they still are, along with "bundlers" and other large campaign contributors in significant policy positions.[34]

Liberals and the media made a mantra of the politics of denigration as the special province of Bush-Cheney-Rove. The Obama record in this regard suggests that Mr. Dooley's "politics-ain't-beanbag" dictum surmounts the constraints of time or party. A critic spoke of the administration's "enemies list," and the frequency with which Obama reminded his listeners that he had inherited the nation's ills from his predecessor became fodder for TV comedians.[35]

The White House has turned its guns on unrestrained critics such as Fox News and Rush Limbaugh and on pollsters for coming up with disappointing public opinion results. These assaults had short lives, as tenuous as their efficacy. Embarrassing, too, are the excesses of Obama's more unrestrained boosters. Vice President Joe Biden, who at times seems type-cast from his counterpart in the Gershwins' *Of Thee I Sing*, is a reliable source. The head of the National Endowment for the Arts caused a minor flap when he called on the Endowment's beneficiaries "to celebrate how the arts can be used for positive change."[36]

Bush's Department of Justice came under liberal fire for appointing off-the-charts reactionaries, condoning torture, and seeking to get rid of United States attorneys for political reasons. Obama's Justice Department and Attorney General Eric Holder have been criticized for appointing off-the-charts radicals, quashing charges against groups such as the New Black Panthers and ACORN, and channeling terrorists to civil trials: counterparts to the charges against the Bush DOJ, but from the other side of the ideological spectrum. This suggests that the office of the attorney general remains a likely source of excess in the modern American state, a view enforced by past instances of controversial AGs stretching from Wilson's A. Mitchell Palmer to Nixon's Edwin Meese, Clinton's Janet Reno, and Bush's John Ashcroft.[37]

INTEREST GROUPS

One of the defining characteristics of American government in the course of the past half century has been the rise of a multitude of special interest and advocacy

groups. Core economic interests—business and commerce, agriculture and industry, veterans and labor—
have interacted with the American state from its earliest
days. Now they have been supplemented by a rich variety
of groups advocating more particular, and less concretely
material, issues: race and gender, environmentalism and
energy, abortion and sexual diversity.

This is not to say that when push comes to shove, the
old interests fail to command the attention of elected
officials and bureaucrats. But the range of new causes
and their political vitality is a significant new force in
American public life. Advocacy groups have substantially extended the public agenda. It may also be said
that their often-rigid goals and their distance from the
give-and-take of party politics have contributed to the
polarization of American politics, and have made it
more difficult to get anything done.

The Obama administration came into office with a
special remit to respond to these new voices. That "the
ways of Washington must change" was a mantra of the
campaign. Along with his core support from blacks, college students, and affluent liberals, Obama's election
seemed to mark the new advocacy groups' coming of
political age.

Among the older groups, organized labor has won a
more sympathetic government response (though not as
much as it expected). Blacks, women, the academic-
think tank Left, and public employees have seen a new
birth of preference. Education and green technology are

well looked after; old standbys such as veterans, oil and gas, manufacturing, and Israel, less so.

Yet here, as elsewhere, there is more than a hint of new wine being poured into old wineskins. It is difficult to distinguish the scale and special-interest impact of political contributions by organized labor (the auto workers', teachers', and service employees' unions in particular) and trial lawyers from the Bushes' oil and gas men. Now as then, those who pay the piper get to have a say in selecting the policy tune, or even to survive. Heavy Democratic contributors AIG and Goldman Sachs were bailed out to wheel and deal another day. Light contributor (and ultimately bankrupt) Lehman Brothers was not.[38]

As the first stage of the Obama administration nears its end, it is difficult to see profound changes in how the business of American government is conducted. That the Obamaites are committed to change is clear. That they have the know-how, or the system has the flexibility, to enable them to achieve their ends is, to put it gently, as yet unresolved.

2

CHAPTER

Fixing the Economy

IT IS SEDUCTIVELY EASY to draw parallels between the Great Depression of the early 1930s and
the Great Recession of the late 2000s. Each had a
severe stock market slump, a banking-financial crisis,
and a major surge in unemployment. And in both cases
a charismatic new president, pledged to change the political and policy environment, succeeded a tired, unpopular incumbent.

The virtues of free markets and slack government
came under fire then as now. Politicians lashed out at
greedy bankers and financiers: the CEOs of Chase,
National City, J.P. Morgan, and the New York Stock
Exchange in the early 1930s; the CEOs of Goldman
Sachs, Bank of America, and AIG in 2008–2009. Con-
venient devil figures fed public outrage: Samuel Insull
and Andrew Mellon then, the stunningly type-cast
Bernie Madoff now. Widely read economists such as
Stuart Chase (a source of the "New Deal" label attached

to FDR's administration) floated collectivist proposals much as Paul Krugman and Joseph Stiglitz do today.[1]

As the Recession of 2008–2009 unfolded, economists debated policy in terms that would have been quite familiar three quarters of a century before. The character and efficacy of regulation, the relationship between recovery and reform, the relative impact of reduced or expanded government spending and taxation: these issues divided market and collectivist economists then as now. The Keynesian quandary of the 1930s—to what degree should, or can, economic recovery rest on a government stimulus?—has re-emerged after decades of quiescence.[2]

As conditions improved, however haltingly, under the New Deal, talk of major structural change—nationalization of the banks, government ownership or direction of industry—faded away. Columnist Walter Lippmann, who thought Roosevelt's was "an administration which disbelieves in the capitalist system," concluded in 1935: "The idea of a planned economy, which swept the country like a fad in 1933, is discredited." Much the same happened over the course of 2009.[3]

One big difference that distinguishes the present from the early 1930s: the consciousness today of the Great Depression not as a mysterious, frightening, unfolding event, but as a heavily analyzed episode in the American past. In this sense the Depression was not unlike World War I: a benchmark that shaped the response to future wars (or, in this case, economic slumps).

The great difference, of course, is the outsized disparity of scale that distinguishes the Great Depression from the Great Recession. In the number of unemployed and the degree of shock to the American social system, the current downturn has been much less severe than the Depression of 1930–1933, or even the slump of 1937–1938. Today's malaise perhaps most resembles the recession of 1973–1975, the prelude to Jimmy Carter's 1976 victory.[4]

But the ultimate character of the current reversal is not yet known. The scale and persistence of unemployment has outstripped most predictions; its end, and overall size, are still to be determined. Stagflation, that unsettling mix of rising prices and rising joblessness, flummoxed the experts in the 1970s. Now a rise in recovery indicators and the stock market on one hand, and persistent unemployment on the other, has restored the sense that we are in new and uncharted economic territory.

BAILING OUT THE BANKS: 1932–1933 AND 2008–2009

The responses to the financial challenges of their times by the Hoover and FDR administrations then and the Bush and Obama administrations now have a number of surface similarities. The Bush-Obama effort in 2008–2009 to deal with an imminent fiscal/banking crisis closely resembles the Hoover-FDR sequence of late 1932 and early 1933. In both cases there was an interval of joint action in the face of a national crisis. And now, as then, the tensions inherent in a change of administrations made this amity a short-lived thing.

Pressure mounted on lame-duck incumbent Herbert Hoover in late 1932 and early 1933 to declare a bank holiday to stanch the rising flow of bank closings. But he refused to do so—at least not without the participation of President-elect Roosevelt. That wily politician was not about to pull Hoover's chestnuts out of the fire. According to his wife Eleanor, when at a meeting of the two men Hoover proposed a joint proclamation, FDR replied: "Like hell I will! If you haven't the guts to do it yourself, I'll wait until I'm president to do it."

And that's what he did. As soon as FDR was sworn in, his chief aide Raymond Moley and Treasury Secretary-designate William Woodin met with outgoing Hoover Treasury chief Ogden Mills and his associates. Moley and Woodin agreed to Mills's idea to proclaim a four-day national bank holiday. Indeed, a bill to that effect (which Mills wanted and Hoover refused to agree to) existed in draft form. Hoover's name was scratched out, FDR's added, and the bill quickly and effortlessly passed through Congress. FDR signed the act seven hours after it was introduced.

Obama's sure-footed initial reaction to the October 2008 banking and financial crisis, and the Hooverlike passivity of John McCain, set the stage for a replay of the March 1933 mini-drama, though this time with the support of the outgoing president. Federal Reserve chief Ben Bernanke (who had written authoritatively on financial policy and the Great Depression) and Bush's

Treasury Secretary Henry Paulson dealt with Obama's economic point man Larry Summers and Treasury-designate Timothy Geithner in a spirit of comparable expedition, and even more collaboratively. Before the new administration (and Congress) took office, they agreed on the near-$700 billion bailout structure embodied in the Troubled Asset Relief Program (TARP), which a reluctant Congress passed and Bush signed.

In 1933 as in 2009, populist-minded legislators bitterly resented what they regarded as a rescue of the financial interests responsible for the mess in which the nation found itself. One congressman observed in 1933: "The President drove the money-changers out of the Capitol on March 4th [in his Inaugural]—and they were all back on the 9th [when the Banking Act became law]." Similar grumbling from both sides of the aisle accompanied the passage of TARP.

For all their differences in ideological, political, and social backgrounds, FDR and Obama had strikingly similar responses to their respective bank crises. Neither heeded calls from the Left—Rexford Tugwell then, Paul Krugman now—to nationalize the banking system. This makes clear the degree to which, in the American political culture, the inclination to preserve or repair existing institutions finesses the impulse, however alluring, for foundational change.

But if conditions are parlous enough, a lesser degree of adaptation is very much in the cards. FDR came into office with well-honed conservative views on economic policy. He was as entrenched in the prevailing early twentieth-century conservative Democratic belief in small government and fiscal prudence as Obama was in early twenty-first century Democratic social liberalism.

He made ur-conservative Lewis Douglas his (for a while, quite influential) director of the budget. One of FDR's first legislative priorities, reflecting a major campaign theme, was a Budget Act that imposed Draconian cuts on federal employees' salaries and veterans' bonus payments. And initially he opposed deposit insurance. Indeed, Roosevelt's expectation when he convened a special session of Congress in the wake of his March 4, 1933 inauguration was that it would adjourn after passing the banking and budget-cutting acts and legalizing more potent beer.

But the political and ideological firestorm stirred by the Great Depression quickly led FDR to confront new realities in fresh ways. Supporters of the view that if it does not repeat itself, history at least rhymes, might savor the fact that seventy-five years before Rahm Emanuel gained a measure of immortality with his admonition five days after the election: "Never allow a crisis to go to waste. They [*sic*] are opportunities to do big things," columnist and pundit Walter Lippmann took note that "there are good crises and there are bad crises." He thought the banking crisis was a good one because it allowed FDR to push for fundamental reform.[5]

For all his antecedents in the Left-liberal social politics of 1990s Chicago, Obama—like FDR—initially backed moderate economic policies. He did not listen to Left economists Krugman, Stiglitz, or Jeffrey Sachs.

Instead, the most influential voices were more mainstream types: Austan Goolsbee and Lawrence Summers, Treasury Secretary Timothy Geithner, Council of Economic Advisers chair Christina Romer.

Did Obama, in retrospect, let his game-changing crisis go to waste? While a few investment firms—Lehman, Bear Stearns, Merrill Lynch—no longer figure (or disfigure) the financial landscape, it must be said, as could be said of the 1930s, that change was limited. Most of the toxic apparatus of the 2000s bubble—collateralized mortgage, loan, and debt obligations, the ambiguously public-private role of Fannie Mae and Freddie Mac—remains very much there. Bankers and brokers continue to scoop up outsized bonuses despite their fingernail-on-the-blackboard effect on the public. Summers took note in mid-October 2009 of as large a disjunction as he had ever seen between the financial sector and the American middle class.[6]

THEN: RELIEF, RECOVERY, AND PUBLIC WORKS

The Great Depression's unrelentingly grim reality— economic stagnation, massive unemployment, skeletal state and local relief overwhelmed by the scale of the disaster—eroded the embedded policy assumptions of pre-Depression America. The new order quickly began to make a legislative mark. First came the Civilian Conservation Corps (CCC) Act of March 31, 1933, grounded in Progressive-era conservation and the World War I army model of administration. It put 250,000 young men to work planting trees and combating soil erosion in four months, and prohibited the exclusion (but not the segregation) of African-Americans within its ranks.

It was in May, when the new administration had been in office for two months, that the policy earthquake triggered by the Depression and FDR's election came into full force. The rural-agricultural sector was the first to win attention. The CCC was followed by the Agricultural Adjustment Authority (AAA), aimed at kick-starting a rise in food prices by restricting production, and the Tennessee Valley Authority (TVA), designed to bring electricity and better farming practices to a physically and socially exhausted region.

On May 12, the same day that the AAA was enacted, the Federal Emergency Relief Administration (FERA) launched the New Deal on its most distinctive and lasting response to the Depression: the dual policies of relief and public works. It would be followed a month later by the Public Works Administration (PWA), part of the National Recovery Act, whose National Recovery Administration (NRA) was the industrial counterpart to the AAA. The Civil Works Administration (CWA) followed in November and the Works Progress Administration (WPA) in 1935. These were the core New Deal responses to the massive unemployment that was the most visible and socially harmful consequence of the Great Depression: the stimulus package of the 1930s.

There was no existing framework for federal relief and public works beyond President Hoover's pioneering Emergency Relief Act of 1932. Basic questions of financing and administration had to be faced. FERA was allocated $500 million, to be treated as a one-off emergency cost rather than a normal government expenditure, and hence off-budget. It would be administered by the states.

Allocation and oversight were in the hands not of Hoover's stodgy and bureaucratic Reconstruction Finance Commission, but a small (121 employees at its peak) and tightly run staff headed by a dynamic, elemental force: Harry Hopkins. In the first two hours after he took charge, Hopkins doled out over $5 million to eight states. During its first year, FERA supported an estimated 17 million needy Americans. By the time it ended in 1935, it had helped 20 million people—16 percent of the population—at a cost of $3.1 billion.

Harold Ickes's Public Works Administration was a significant player in its own, different way. The $3.3 billion allocated to it under the National Recovery Act in 1933 was 165 percent of the federal government's 1933 revenue and about 6 percent of GDP. PWA projects were strategically placed in 2,068 of the country's 3,071 counties. Boulder Dam, TVA, 78,000 bridges, about 40,000 post offices and other public buildings, and the aircraft carriers that were crucial in the aftermath of Pearl Harbor were the PWA's major legacies.

Its role in easing Depression-era unemployment is less clear. PWA focused on architects, engineers, and skilled construction workers: not conducive to large-scale job creation. Indeed, the PWA's impact on the length of the Depression may well have been to extend rather than to shorten it. But its contribution to the nation's infrastructure was substantial. In this sense it is the predecessor of the new technology infrastructure objectives that are part of Obama's stimulus package.

The Civil Works Administration had a more immediate spinoff. As the winter of 1933–1934 approached, it became apparent that the slow-moving PWA, run by the pathologically honest Harold Ickes, was not creating jobs with sufficient speed and in sufficient numbers. CWA, run by Hopkins, poured unallocated PWA funds into immediate construction jobs: 800,000 in ten days, two million in two weeks, four million in fifty days. This came at a high cost: about a billion dollars in five months, compared to an initial estimate of $400 million. Ickes (for bureaucratic turf reasons) and Budget Director Douglas (for ideological reasons) got CWA closed down in March 1934. But the millions of jobs eased the pain of the winter. And the roads, schools, playgrounds, sewers (and 250,000 outhouses) built by CWA set the pattern for New Deal public works to come.

WPA, the final New Deal unemployment relief agency, was designed to concentrate on more varied projects (including, famously, support for artists and writers). It too was generously funded: 135 percent of federal revenue, 6.7 percent of GDP in 1936. It was also by far the most contentious—a measure of the limited public-political capacity to countenance work relief once the threat of social disaster passed.

WPA employed 3.3 million people in late 1937, half working on roads and highways. Its payroll was among the nation's biggest; indeed, U.S. welfare spending was the largest in the world. A wave of charges of useless make-work and corruption, and of left-wing politics infesting its arts and writing programs, swept over WPA (though some of its critics might have found solace in the knowledge that in its final years, WPA built the Japanese-American relocation camps). Graft and bribery in fact were inconsequential. But patronage and party politics were not. At one point, over 90 percent of Pittsburgh's Democratic ward committeemen were WPA foremen.[7]

NOW: STIMULUS AND BUDGET

What insights into the Obama administration's job-stimulus effort are provided by these New Deal analogues? In its scale, the $787 billion (soon to cost a trillion and more) American Economic Recovery and Reinvestment Act of 2009 was about 6 percent of the nation's $14.2 trillion GDP; proportionately a bit less than the PWA and WPA expenditures, but not by much. In its sense of urgency, too, Obama's stimulus echoed FDR's employment relief. Dire warnings as to the consequences of delay sped it along. The conference committee's report was introduced in the House at 1 a.m. on

February 13, 2009; the bill was passed later that day after an hour of debate and by the Senate sixteen hours after that. Shades of the Hundred Days!

The initial reaction to the Stimulus Act was positive. The need to do something was evident, and almost everyone could find something to like. Reaganite economist Lawrence Kudlow praised Obama's initial package, proposed in early January before the inauguration, because it included $300 billion in tax cuts. Obama's economic gurus Summers, Geithner, Romer, and Goolsbee welcomed the spur to the economy that the tax cuts promised to provide.

House Majority Leader Steny Hoyer predicted that the Stimulus Act would apply an "immediate jolt" to the economy. Summers declared, "You'll see the effects almost immediately." Budget Director Peter Orszag foresaw "only weeks or months" to wait. Two million jobs "created or saved" became a political mantra, along with dire warnings of a rise in unemployment to 8 percent if no stimulus package were passed.[8]

In one important respect, Obama's stimulus differed sharply from FDR's work relief programs. PWA, CWA, and WPA were the creations of FDR and his New Dealers. Of course the interests of members of Congress and their constituents were noted. But Harold Ickes and Harry Hopkins put their own distinctive stamps on these programs.

Why did Obama forego a similar approach? Why did he turn over his stimulus bill to the none-too-tender mercies of Speaker Nancy Pelosi and Appropriations

Chair David Obey? Instead of being shaped by a strong director responsible to the White House, the stimulus bill was a 1,071-page dog's breakfast: a long wish list of liberal projects (such as negating a portion of Bill Clinton's 1996 welfare reform act) and local pork, seasoned by the $300 billion in tax cuts.

The most obvious answers are that the crisis of 1933–1934 was far greater than the crisis of 2008–2009, and that Congress, the president, and the party system in 1933 had a different character, and different relations to one another, than was the case in 2009. The parties and the president then had more authority, Congress members less autonomy. Today the average member of Congress is in effect an individual entrepreneur whose fund-raising, longevity in office, and election prowess rest more heavily on his or her own organization and clout than on the party or the president. The Stimulus Act in effect reflected that new, large fact of American political life.

Clinton, too, had proposed a stimulus bill when he came into office in 1993, but of very different scale and political consequence. He sought "an ambitious set of programs that would infuse federal funds into the economy to jump-start a recovery. The economic stimulus package, as it came to be called, consumed a great deal of the administration's time and effort in the early months."

Clinton's $16.3 billion package passed swiftly through the House but bogged down in the Senate, where forty-two of the forty-three Republicans threatened a filibuster and blocked cloture. Clinton finally had to content himself with a $4 billion extension of unemployment benefits.[9]

Obama's Stimulus Act was an altogether larger and more broad-based measure. About a third was devoted to tax cuts, aimed at particular targets such as energy-related home improvements and first-time home buyers. It also expanded the earned income tax credit. It did not reduce corporate and payroll taxes, which the conservative-minded saw as the high road to recovery.

Another third consisted of aid to state and local governments: a genuflection to the public service unions who contributed so handsomely to Obama's campaign and a convenient way for Congress to take care of its own (that is, its own constituents).

The final third was devoted to upgrading and modernizing the nation's infrastructure. Only a modest 10 percent was allocated to the highway and similar improvements that were at the core of the New Deal's programs. An independent, bipartisan oversight board was supposed to make sure that stimulus funds were spent wisely and well.

The first anniversary of the Stimulus Act in February 2010 kicked off a debate over its efficacy. Most expert observers (including the Congressional Budget Office) put its job-creating-or-saving impact at between 1.6 million and 1.8 million. But a CBS/New York Times poll found that only 6 percent of respondents thought the stimulus had in fact created new jobs. And the unemployment rate of around 10 percent was considerably higher even than the 8 percent that the administration forecast if no stimulus were in place. This was in stark contrast to the first years of the New Deal, when the jobless rate did indeed fall substantially. (But then it had so much further to fall.)

By the end of its first year, about a third of the stimulus funds had been spent. One supporter conceded that expenditures on roads, buildings, and other visible projects were "a bit sluggish." Those who were inclined to look upon the stimulus and find it good, found it good. Those who weren't, didn't.[10]

Stimulus infrastructure projects were scheduled to pick up in 2010. Seventy percent of the stimulus budget was to be spent by October (which, it may be noted, precedes the election month of November). In this, at least, stimulus spending echoes the New Deal's public works, which also were expended with an eye or two cocked to election day.

Facts of American life that make the Great Recession so different from the Great Depression are at play here. Among them is the existence of unemployment compensation and other welfare props that make joblessness less of a social disaster. But firms are demonstrating an unexpected capacity to increase their productivity without rehiring laid-off workers.

Obama and his people expected more from the stimulus than it could deliver. Critics from the Left hold that it was not large enough to make a difference. A third perspective—that the American economy is more subject to the vagaries of the market than to public policy–perhaps trumps both of those assumptions.

■ ■ ■

Another measure of the differing intensities of the Great Depression and the Great Recession was the greater degree of popular support for FERA, PWA, and even WPA than for the Stimulus Act. For all the sense of urgency with which Obama sold his program, its commitment to long-term liberal Democratic goals led to an all but straight party-line vote. No Republicans in the House and only three in the Senate (Maine's moderate women and soon-to-become Democrat Arlen Specter of Pennsylvania) supported the bill: a preview of what awaited Obama's health care.

The heightened partisanship of modern American politics ensured GOP obduracy. The contrast with TARP—which, like the 1933 bank holiday, benefited from the easier bipartisanship of a presidential transition period—is dramatic.

The question remains: Why did a new president, much of whose appeal lay in his campaign pledge to bring a less partisan culture to Washington, plunge so rapidly into so divisive a policy approach? Why did he let the congressional Democratic leadership call the turn on his program's substance and tactics?

Obama's stance echoed that of Bush: a tropistic turn to his party's more ideological elements, even though the bulk of evidence suggested that centrist moderation was what a plurality of voters wanted. Pundits, the media culture, the political class, advocacy groups, moneyed interests: all fostered a mode of politics that appealed to the tails of a primarily moderate public opinion bell curve. Neither Bush nor Obama appeared to be able to go beyond the rhetorical in surmounting this state of affairs.

RELIEF VERSUS RECOVERY

Obama's New Foundation, like FDR's New Deal, juggled two major, and in many ways conflicting, policy goals: to deal with the politically toxic issue of unemployment and to respond to the challenge of putting the nation on the road to a revived and updated economy.

From the first, the New Deal pursued the twin goals of relief and recovery. CCC put young men to work by planting trees and thus (to throw in a mixed metaphor) sow the seeds for a more fruitful land. TVA put men to work building dams, while seeking to restore the soil and social well-being of a benighted region. AAA and NRA were designed not only to get farms and factories, farmers and workers through the grim present, but to restructure agriculture and industry through production and price controls. CWA, PWA, and WPA sought not only to put men to work but to leave behind a legacy of tangible accomplishments—public buildings, dams, bridges, an enhanced military infrastructure—that would change the face of the nation.

The Obama administration has been driven by a similar set of objectives. The Stimulus Act was offered as a quick fix to the 2008–2009 surge in joblessness. But along with traditional New Deal-style relief and public works (keeping public employees on the job, fixing roads and other infrastructure) was a healthy component of New Age objectives: as Appropriations chair Obey grandly put it, "to transform our economy with science and technology."[11]

This second goal became more evident when in February 2009 the administration offered up a $3.55 trillion eye-opener of a 2010 budget and projected a fiscal 2009 deficit of $4 trillion: 27.7 percent of GDP, compared to 20 percent in 2007 and 21 percent in 2008.

The 2010 budget gave government spending the highest share of the economy since 1945, and foresaw only a light falloff for the rest of the decade. (The $3.69 trillion 2011 budget, proposed a year later, made it clear that this new height was a plateau and not a summit.) If money talks (and budgets indeed are a form of discourse), then this was a loquacious declaration of intent.

In point of fact, nearly two thirds of the 2010 expenditure was committed before Obama arrived on the scene: to Social Security, Medicare and Medicaid, and the Department of Defense. But the far-from-insignificant residue of $1.3 trillion represented major policy commitments, especially when combined with the substantial Stimulus Act allocations to the same departments and programs.

The stimulus added little to the budgets of agencies whose missions were not central to the vision of the New Foundation: Defense, State, Veterans Affairs, Homeland Security, NASA. But the departments of Transportation and Housing and Urban Development and the Environmental Protection Agency benefited substantially. A

170 percent-larger $81.1 billion stimulus add-on to Education's $46.7 billion budget, a 147 percent hike of $38.7 billion to Energy's $46.7 billion budget, and a doubling of Labor's $13.3 billion added up to substantial funding for Obama's New Foundation. This was a massive commitment to environmental protection, a new effort at urban rehabilitation, new energy-saving forms of transportation, publicly subsidized housing and education, and benefits to labor.[12]

So far these objectives have not matched the political appeal of the New Deal's public works agenda. The Stimulus Act never won widespread public acceptance. Rather than being seen as the expression of a large vision for the American future, the Obama economic proposals found it difficult to transcend the taint of pork, waste, and ineffectiveness that so many Americans so often attach to the workings of government. In August 2009, 43 percent of those polled thought the Stimulus Act was a bad idea; only a third supported it.[13]

Federalism, as it does so often, reared its ugly head. The interests, rules, and customs of states and localities did not always coincide with federal objectives. Substantial awards to teachers and other public employees hardly strengthened the politics of the stimulus. State-federal agency disputes flared over the use of funds. Kansas wanted to save more of its allocation than the feds thought was called for; Texas spent a tenth of its transportation funding for highway improvements in the Houston area, thus fostering the liberal no-no of dependence on oil.[14]

Environmentalists had a strong distaste for the infrastructure projects that were the most "job-ready" and publicly acceptable realm of expenditure. (By August 2009, more than 7,000 transportation projects had been approved.) Obama's science adviser John Holdren did not buttress the cause of getting the nation back to work when it emerged that he had once lent his support to "de-development."[15]

And anecdotalism did its corrosive work (as it had with the WPA's "leaf-raking"). On the same day that New York's Senator Charles Schumer complained that a billion stimulus dollars had been spent to buy windmill energy blades from an overseas firm, the Department of Labor reported a substantial increase in aid applications from workers and businesses displaced by foreign competition.[16]

As the Stimulus Act unfolded, it drifted ever further from the New Deal's PWA-CWA-WPA model. Put forward as a quick-response fix to unemployment, it was supposed to have spent a third of its total in the first six months after enactment. But only about a tenth—roughly $70 billion—had been allocated by July 24. To meet the initial goal, a billion dollars a day would have to be spent during the next four weeks.

Quick fixes such as "cash for clunkers," "cash for caulkers," and subsidies for first-time mortgagees did not—could not—significantly affect the larger jobs market. An embarrassing, and revealing, crossed-signals episode occurred when Council of Economic Advisers head Christine Romer declared that the jobs-creating role of the Stimulus Act was pretty much limited to the first half of 2009, while economics adviser Summers predicted that it would peak in the second half. Nor did it help when in October 2009 an attempt to gather job-creation data collapsed into a welter of fabricated facts, invented congressional districts, and other displays of bureaucratic deception, illusionism, and incompetence. In the 1930s the Bureau of Labor Statistics did not regard those working on New Deal relief projects as employed; in 2010, short-term Census workers were so counted.[17]

Through Obama's first year the jobs picture remained bleak, and talk rose of a second injection of government funds. It was called not a stimulus but a "jobs package." While economist Paul Krugman and others of the Left held that a substantially larger stimulus was what the doctor ordered, public opinion weighed against it. In a rare burst of bipartisanship, senators from the two parties came up with a new jobs bill and the White House signaled its approval. But Senate Majority Leader Harry Reid, for (unclear) reasons of his own, proposed a pared-down substitute in its stead.[18]

Perhaps the most significant consequence of the stimulus was that it encouraged Obama and his associates to conclude that the employment crisis was well in hand and that they were free to turn their attention to more toothsome applications of the New Foundation such as recasting the American health care system.

LABOR AND UNIONS

Its interplay with organized labor was of major importance to the New Deal's political and legislative evolu-
tion. Rapidly growing industrial unions, particularly
those of the new Congress of Industrial Organizations (CIO), were among the primary political building
blocks of FDR's electoral coalition. And some of the
New Deal's major legislative acts were milestones in
American labor history. These included section 7A of
the National Industrial Recovery Act (which gave a
green light to industrial unionization), the National
Labor Relations Act (the Wagner Act), and the Fair
Labor Standards Act. The latter two made collective
bargaining over wages and hours between employers
and unions an integral part of American industrial
labor relations.[19]

This was a tough—indeed, an impossible—act for
Obama to follow. Large-scale industrial unions now are
not a movement waiting to be born, but a venerable institution in what looks like terminal decline. By 2010
only about 7 percent of the non-public workforce belonged to unions, and there was little prospect of a
revival.

Public unions were another story: they enrolled 38 percent of the government workforce. The National Education Association (NEA), the American Federation of
Teachers (AFT) and the American Federation of State,
County, and Municipal Employees (AFSCME), along
with the Service Employees International Union (SEIU),

one of the few thriving primarily non-public labor organizations, were major supporters of the Obama election campaign, seriously generous with money and workers. An end to the secret ballot requirement for unionization was the non-public union leaders' most cherished hope of revival. This cause bogged down in a swamp of congressional and administration indifference. But Obama did what he could for the United Auto Workers, the major private industry union. The largest non-financial bailout under TARP involved General Motors and Chrysler, who faced bankruptcy because of mediocre sales and onerous payroll, pension, and health care obligations. Despite limited public support, Obama moved forcefully to spare the companies the rigors of full-scale bankruptcy and saw to it that the bulk of the cost was borne not by the workers but by bondholders. Indeed, the UAW wound up a large-scale stockholder in both firms.

Public employee unions would be even more substantial beneficiaries of government largesse. The biggest portion of the stimulus went in its first year to the public sector, in effect sustaining the state and local expansion of the boom years. Among the beneficiaries: 325,000 teachers. What would happen when this booster charge ran down remained unclear, even after Congress voted an additional $26 billion in August 2010 to maintain the jobs of teachers and other state employees.[20]

As the Obama regime unfolds, the larger question of the place of unions in American life remains. Public indifference to the plight of the auto workers was hardly lessened by the UAW's favorable treatment in the auto bailout or by the attempt to exempt members' "Cadillac" health plans from additional taxation. And evidence mounted that the sizable employment, salary, health benefits, and—most of all—pensions of state and (less so) federal employees were becoming a potent source of public anger.[21]

REGULATING THE FINANCIAL SYSTEM

Along with relief and recovery, the New Deal turned its attention to regulating the nation's banking and financial systems. Its achievements were as notable as the jobs-creation and public works of the PWA, CWA, and WPA. Federal deposit insurance, the Securities and Exchange Commission (SEC), and the Glass-Steagall Act, which separated deposit from investment banking, added up to a system of oversight that functioned well enough for the next fifty years.[22]

Here again, Obama's New Foundation started not from ground zero but with a substantial and mature regulatory system in place. (For example: one problem was not the lack of a securities regulatory agency, but what to do about an SEC asleep at the switch.)

It appeared to be as easy, and as politically profitable, for the Obama administration to indulge in populist banker-bashing in 2009–2010 as it had been for FDR in the 1930s. But now there were complications that FDR didn't have to face. One was the involvement—some would say the complicity—of the government in the practices that led to the real estate mortgage bubble and the ensuing property, banking, and investment collapses. Obama tried manfully to fix the blame for these failures on big investment firms, insurers, and national banks: on Goldman Sachs, AIG, Chase, Bank of America. But key figures on his economic team—Treasury Secretary Geithner, economics adviser Summers, Federal Reserve Chairman Bernanke—were hardly uninvolved in the policies, or the institutions, implicated in the 2008 implosion.

In June 2009 Obama launched "a sweeping overhaul of the financial regulatory system, a transformation not seen since the reforms that followed the Great Depression." As in the case of his response to unemployment, he had the New Deal model of bold, large-scale action very much in mind. But his reforms had to cover not only deposit-commercial and investment banking but a massive credit-card market all but nonexistent in the 1930s, and a host of new and strange denizens in the financial deeps such as hedge funds and a bewildering array of investment instruments generically known as derivatives. In May 2009 an overwhelming congressional majority passed a crackdown on the credit-card industry's interest and other practices: about as popular a regulatory add-on as can be imagined.[23]

Other financial realms were more contentious. A comprehensive regulatory overhaul was slated to appear by mid-June 2009. Obama hoped to be able to sign his bill into law by the end of the year. Soon enough this cause became another reminder that 2009 was not 1933, and that Obama and the New Foundation were not FDR and the New Deal.

In its initial form, Obama's financial plan was a modest eighty-eight-page document: barely an introduction by modern bill-drafting standards. It proposed a new agency to protect the consumers of financial products and sought to impose greater (or at least some) transparency on derivatives trading. But its larger purpose was to patch up a regulatory system already in place.

As the first Obama year unfolded, the question of how to handle the financial structure became enmeshed in a web of obstacles not unlike those entwining health care. Much of the difficulty lay not so much in the size of the Democratic congressional majority, or a lack of public support, but in the sheer scale of the existing framework of government agencies, vested interests, and advocacy groups.

Former Federal Reserve chair Paul Volcker, drafted by Obama to head an Economic Recovery Advisory Board, proposed that the biggest banks be broken up and Glass-Steagall's separation of savings from investment banking (ended in 1999) be restored. Initially he was shunted aside by the more influential (and more big-bank-sympathetic) Geithner-Summers-Orszag trio. Asked if he was losing influence, Volcker replied: "I did not have influence to start with." Adherence to the "too big to fail" dogma saved Chase, Bank of America, AIG, and Goldman Sachs—but not Lehman Brothers and Bear Stearns.[24]

And then there was the Fannie Mae-Freddie Mac problem. The administration with some justification could hang responsibility on the Bush administration for too-low mortgage interest rates and too-slack oversight of sleight-of-hand mortgage packaging and loose banking and investment practices. But the substantial contribution of quasi-governmental Fannie Mae and Freddie Mac to the mortgage bubble, prodded by Democratic representatives such as Barney Frank, to assist under- (or non-) qualified home buyers, blurred the simplistic picture of a complicit Bush administration and a pure-as-snow Democratic opposition.

When the financial storm hit in late 2008, Fannie and Freddie were included in the too-big-to-fail TARP bailout. As those institutions continued to stagger under the weight of their accumulated bad-mortgage obligations, the administration stepped in to turn the temporary TARP prop into a more permanent one. It agreed to absorb whatever losses the mortgage giants incurred during the next three years. Republicans called on the government to permanently assume their obligations (and thereby add another fillip to the already distended deficit). As of mid-May 2010, $145 billion in government bailout money had gone to prop up the ailing firms.

Were Fannie and Freddie now full-bore responsibilities of the government? The Obama administration's interventionist inclination, and the role of mortgage-provider of last resort that the progressive-minded saw for Fannie and Freddie, supported such an understanding. Political reality counseled otherwise.[25]

In compliance with the inexorable laws of politics and government, the very scope of the Obama regulatory reforms touched off turf wars. And there were many more players than in 1933. Obama proposed that the Federal Reserve's regulatory and oversight power be expanded so that it could act as the chief overseer of risk in the financial system. But Senate Banking Committee Chair Christopher Dodd wanted to reduce the Fed's supervisory authority. When in February 2010 Dodd announced his intention to retire, his clout diminished.[26]

Other agencies and individuals with ambitions stoked by the new administration's green light to assertive government wanted larger slices of the regulatory pie. These included the Treasury, the Federal Deposit Insurance Corporation headed by the ambitious Sheila Bair, the Securities Exchange Commission, and Comptroller of the Currency John Dugan. The SEC, with support in the Senate Banking Committee, opposed a super-regulator for consumer financial products. The big public pension funds—another key player now, unknown in the early 1930s—also opposed any reduction in the SEC's power. But an SEC merger with the Commodity Futures Trading Commission, which regulated derivatives, was likely to be opposed by the House and Senate agriculture committees. A consultant summed up the situation: "Everyone is fighting everyone."[27]

By early 2010 Democratic election defeats and the bruising health care battle had taken much of the starch out of the Obama program, and his financial bill languished. Congress toyed with proposals to improve the character and performance of corporate governance. Dodd and the GOP's Bob Corker of Tennessee were supposed to work together on a financial regulation bill.

But in the wake of the passage of Obamacare, financial regulation got a new lease on life. The Dodd-Frank Wall Street Reform and Consumer Protection Act, as grandiose in length (2,319 pages) as in name, slowly made its way through Congress, winning passage and Obama's signature in July 2010.

Financial reform's legislative profile and history bore a striking resemblance to those of its health care predecessor. Once again, the party's congressional leadership—in this case Dodd of Connecticut and Frank of Massachusetts—crafted a bill that reflected the party's liberal-populist bent. And once again it was repeatedly modified in response to the diverse and influential interests that it sought to regulate.

What finally emerged, with token Republican support, was a bill of great complexity. It sought to further protect consumers of financial products, to more closely regulate large banks, and to limit abuses of such activities as proprietary trading, hedge funds, and private equity holdings.

In this sense Dodd-Frank was in the tradition of the New Deal's Glass-Steagall Act, which for over half a century kept private and commercial banking separate. But there the similarity ended. Dodd-Frank dealt with domestic and international financial concerns of a scope and complexity far beyond Glass-Steagall's simpler, relatively constricted world. And it faced years of regulatory implementation before its full character and impact would emerge.[28]

In sum, the politics and policy of financial reform so closely resembled the politics and policy of health care reform that it is tempting to conclude that they reflect the dominant character of modern American legislation. And while Obama predictably sought to make financial reform, as he did health care reform, part of a larger agenda, there was little reason to think that the public so regarded it. Once again, the programmatic presidency found it difficult to thrive in so atomized, diversely motivated, and institutionally feeble a political environment.

TAXATION

During his campaign, Obama was crystal-clear on two matters of tax policy: the massive expansion of government activity would not be paid for by borrowing alone; the necessary taxation would be levied exclusively on families making $250,000 a year or more. But as 2009 morphed into 2010, it was increasingly likely that these pledges would earn a place in the pantheon of feckless presidential promises next to Bush the Elder's "no new taxes" and the pledge attributed (questionably) to Herbert Hoover of "a chicken in every pot and a car in every garage."

One major problem: there was little reason to think that the 5 percent or so of families in the $250,000-and-up bracket would be able to make up the expected federal shortfall. Nor was it necessarily desirable public policy to have more than half the population pay no federal income taxes while a small segment bore the brunt of the burden. (The top 1 percent of households, who earned 16 percent of national income, already paid 34 percent of federal taxes.)

As it became clear that trillion-dollar-plus deficits were to be a fixed part of the American fiscal scene, pressure grew on Obama to adopt an FDR-like readiness to tax. The New Deal increased income tax rates (especially those of corporations) and added levies on undistributed profits and a Social Security withholding impost. But by Obama's time, tax territory was not so underdeveloped.

His primary targets of opportunity: the Bush cuts on inheritance and high income and estate taxes; levies on out-of-favor industries such as coal and oil; and perhaps a VAT (value-added tax), in effect a national sales tax—an appealing way of fudging his no-income-tax-increase pledge.

But each of these faced political problems of massive proportions. Nor did more limited fixes fare well. An Obama proposal to raise $50 billion over ten years by taxing soft drinks foundered in the face of strong resistance from the beverage companies and a conspicuous lack of public support. A trial balloon to limit the charitable deductions of wealthy taxpayers met with a similar enthusiasm void in Congress. And a proposal to tax the high-end policies of so-called "Cadillac" health insurance policies made no greater progress. Obama aide David Axelrod argued that this would affect "the $40,000 policies that the head of Goldman Sachs has" and "not impact on the middle class." But it would also affect the health policies of union members, who earned considerably less than Goldman execs. The proposal bid fair to be another road to nowhere. Nor did Obama gain much credibility by holding that "health care reform is fiscal reform." Most Americans found it difficult to believe that a massive expansion of health care would produce surplus revenue.[29]

▪ ▪ ▪

As of mid-2010, what can be said of Obama's economic policy, compared to that of the early New Deal? That his response to the Great Recession has not so far redounded to his political advantage, unlike FDR's response to the Great Depression, seems clear. Why this is so needs some explaining.

Nothing in the current American situation—neither the scale nor the social pain of unemployment, or the state of the larger economy—compares to the Depression. FDR's New Deal may be faulted for failing to do much for economic recovery. But there is no denying the scale or impact of its relief and public works programs, its spur to unionization and collective bargaining, or its reforms of the nation's banking and investment institutions. Coupled with its construction of a political coalition unprecedented in range and variety, the New Deal's hold on popular approval during the 1930s is readily understandable.

Obama confronts an economic and political situation only superficially similar to that of FDR. Unemployment has never come close to Depression levels. And there is a welfare-state security blanket that did not exist in the early 1930s. Arguably this has hurt rather than helped him politically. Whether because his Stimulus Act was not large enough, was not used effectively, or could not but be an inadequate response to the problems of so vast and complex an economy, it has not yet made noticeable inroads into joblessness. Obama's reform of the financial system, like his reform of the health care system, is unclear in its character, timetable, and time of impact. And in stark contrast to FDR in 1933 and 1934, his political situation appears to be eroding.

A Clintonian realignment of economic policy that wins wide public acclaim is always within the realm of possibility. (FDR was famous for his flexibility in this regard.) One question about Obama—as was increasingly asked about Roosevelt—is the degree of his commitment to a market-driven system of free enterprise. But just as the depth and sincerity of FDR's free market beliefs were less important than his political sensitivity, so is this likely to be the case with Obama. It may well be that his core belief is in European-style government intervention. His commitment to big spending and whopping deficits suggests that this is so. But at the same time, Obama's lips are in growing service to the tenets of fiscal and budgetary responsibility. How sincere this is may be of less consequence than how economically beneficial and politically necessary it turns out to be.[30]

3
CHAPTER

Into the Maze: Health Care

ARP and the stimulus had only tenuous connec-
tions to New Deal analogues such as the bank
holiday, deposit insurance, and FDR's public
works/relief programs. But when Obama turned to reform of the health care system, the second of his Big
Three causes (energy and cap-and-trade was the third),
he entered a different public policy realm. Obamacare
had two major predecessors of comparable sweep: FDR's
Social Security (1935) and LBJ's Medicare (1965).

LBJ was intensely aware that Social Security was the
jewel in the New Deal's crown. Through Medicare,
along with civil rights, education, and the rest of his
Great Society agenda, he expected to earn a comparable
(indeed, a greater) place in the history of American
liberalism.

Obama saw himself in this tradition. And it was
through his health care proposal that he expected to secure his niche in the social welfare hall of fame beside

FDR and LBJ. After all, neither Harry Truman, nor Jimmy Carter, nor Bill Clinton had been able to secure a system of universal health care. After the enactment of the civil rights legislation of the 1960s and the passage of Medicare, it was the most important remaining building block in the construction of the American welfare state: an appropriate capstone to the New Foundation.[1]

ANALOGY ANNALS

The legislative history of Obamacare, compared to its Social Security, Medicare, and (failed) Hillarycare antecedents, is the tale of a changing society and an evolving system of politics and government interacting with particular interests and the weight of the past.

Obama and his advisers appear to have taken the rapid passage of the Stimulus Act as a signal that his signature program of health care had a green light. They believed that the stimulus would further a recovery already showing some signs of getting under way during the early months of 2009, and that their mantra of millions of jobs to be saved or created was as good as truth.

Political analyst Charlie Cook thought in February 2010 that the commitment to the stimulus had been "one of the biggest miscalculations that we've seen in modern political history." This judgment within a month would be negated by the passage of Obamacare. At the same time, Obamacare turned out to be far more ideologically divisive, partisan, fiscally uncertain, and

programmatically problematical than its major analogues Social Security and Medicare.[2]

▪ ▪ ▪

Roosevelt turned to Social Security not in the first flush
of the early New Deal, but after the 1934 by-election
and an unprecedented increase in the ruling party's congressional representation. It came before a Congress
with Democratic majorities of forty-four in the Senate
and 216 in the House.

Its content was left not to House and Senate committees and their faceless staffs, but to a Committee on Economic Security created in 1934. Headed by Secretary of
Labor Frances Perkins, it included administration heavy-
weights Treasury Secretary Henry Morgenthau, Attorney General Homer Cummings, Henry Wallace of
Agriculture, and Federal Emergency Relief Administra-
tor Harry Hopkins, plus a staff of experts from relevant
federal agencies and a few outside consultants. As in the
case of the New Deal's public works agencies, the committee worked with an effectiveness and expedition un-
imaginable today.

Then as now, Republicans initially set themselves in
opposition. All but one GOP House member voted to
send the bill back to committee. But when that failed,
Social Security glided through Congress with overwhelming bipartisan votes: 372 to thirty-three in the
House and seventy-seven to six in the Senate.

GOP reservations and the potential opposition of
Southern Democrats—the equivalents of today's Blue

Dogs, but far more numerous and powerful—were dealt with by major constraints in the bill. Farm workers and domestic servants were not included, nor were employees in businesses with less than ten employees. An estimated 40 percent of white and 65 percent of black workers were not eligible for Social Security in its initial form.

The program was further removed from the taint of radicalism by being defined as essentially a system of old age and unemployment insurance, its financing based on contributions from employers, employees, and the government. The states, not the federal government, were to administer it.

It was during the post-World War II decades that Social Security became the near-universal entitlement system it is today. Major increases in the scale and benefit level of coverage occurred under GOP presidents Eisenhower and Reagan, as well as under Democrats Truman and Johnson. Its only significant contraction—the Welfare Reform Act of 1996—was signed by Democrat Clinton. From its origins to its maturity, Social Security was as much a national, bipartisan construct as the political system allowed.[3]

▪ ▪ ▪

LBJ's Medicare is the closest social welfare equivalent to FDR's Social Security. This was no accident: among the many things consuming that outsized president was his desire to surpass the New Deal.

In form and function, Medicare closely followed its Social Security prototype. Indeed, it was proposed and passed as an amendment to the Social Security Act. Its core purpose was to provide (compulsory) hospital insurance to Americans aged sixty-five and older. Attached to it was Medicaid: subsidized hospital care for those unable to afford Medicare premiums. As in Social Security, federal grants would go to the states, which shared in the costs and administration of the program. Hospitals (and, in Medicare Part B, doctors) were wooed with the prospect of a vastly larger clientele and the equivalent of toothsome cost-plus contracts with the government.

Like other Great Society programs, Medicare was drafted by a small task force of experts. And as elsewhere, Johnson saw to it that it attracted considerable Republican support. (As he told Hubert Humphrey regarding the Civil Rights Act, "We've got to make this an American bill and not just a Democratic bill.") A majority of the House's Republicans and thirteen of the thirty GOP senators voted for it.

Medicare Part B, which extended the system to include doctors as well as hospitals, was the work of Ways and Means Chair Wilbur Mills, who wanted his share of the glory. This differed from the Social Security-Medicare model: while state-run like the others, it was not compulsory but voluntary. Social Security Commissioner Robert Ball was charged with enticing a sufficient share of the over-sixty-five population to sign up and pay for the program: a challenge not unlike the current issue of how to get the young and healthy to sign up for Obamacare.

Ball, who like many of his counterparts today saw Medicare as the first step to a system of government-run national health insurance, rose brilliantly to this nuts-and-bolts challenge. He used the Post Office, the Internal Revenue Service, unions, and nursing homes to track down and convince potential participants to join. After four months, eight million of fifteen million eligible Americans signed up; in ten months, 90 percent.

The next task was to set up a state-by-state system of private-sector insurance carriers. Again, Ball did not allow his public system leanings to get in the way of doing what had to be done. He worked with members of Congress and other local movers and shakers to craft sets of insurers suitable to each commonwealth, including the larger private insurance companies such as Blue Cross and Blue Shield, group health plans, and coops.[4]

Like the nation's World War II production effort, the implementation of Medicare was swift, effective—and costly. Medicare and Medicaid, its adjunct plan for the poor, enrolled more than 88 million people by 2008, to general satisfaction. But its costs gave every sign of getting out of control: an $813.5 billion bill in 2008 for Medicare and Medicaid combined. Doctors' compensation is inadequately covered by the system; fraud and high administrative costs, and often uninformed and insensitive direction from Washington, afflict it.[5]

■ ■ ■

There are other analogues relevant to Obamacare. One was Jimmy Carter's decision early on to focus (as

Obama was to do with health care) on a touchstone issue. Carter won election in 1976 much as Obama did in 2008: with a campaign that pledged to replace the old partisan, special-interest politics with a more high-minded approach transcending party and parochial concerns. When he came into office, Carter, like Obama, put forward a comprehensive program, including sweeping new health care and energy policies.

Massachusetts Senator Ted Kennedy acidly observed that Carter's reforms "are already lined up bumper to bumper." Carter pledged to take prompt, decisive action on his agenda. But he made energy rather than health care his first priority. (*Congressional Quarterly*: "The first session of the Ninety-fifth Congress could be said to have had two agendas: energy and everything else.") In the oil-embargo 1970s, this was an overriding public concern. As Carter put it, "I have equated energy policy legislation with either success or failure of my first year in office." But energy then, like health care now, did not figure in public opinion polls as a leading issue.

Carter being Carter, he did not stoop to prepare the ground for his energy initiative by reaching out to congressional leaders or potential energy industry allies. Instead, he presented a bill stretching through five telephone-book-sized volumes to an appalled House Speaker Tip O'Neill. Seventeen House committees and subcommittees could claim some jurisdiction. The Speaker created a bipartisan ad hoc committee to avoid that logjam. The House passed the bill in August 1977. It went to the Senate, where five committees squabbled over it; Abraham Ribicoff of Connecticut called the bill "a shambles."

Carter's rhetoric became increasingly hyperbolic. But he failed to marshal public support, as the oil-embargo threat faded away. By late summer a shrinking percentage thought that energy was a major issue. The first year of Carter's term ended with nothing passed. In October 1978, on the eve of the congressional election, a stripped-down version of the original bill was enacted, and signed by Carter. That did not keep the Democrats from a substantial defeat in November.[6]

■ ■ ■

When Bill Clinton became president in 1993, he made universal health care his first major priority. His approach, characteristically, was a mix of the mom-and-pop-store politics and egghead public policy that characterized his and his wife Hillary's climb up politics' greasy pole. Mrs. Clinton was charged with overseeing the drafting of a bill (though her husband's role has not been adequately appreciated). Closed-door hearings with hundreds of health care experts produced legislation requiring employers to cover all of their workers through health maintenance organizations (eventually to become the Democrats' favorite hobgoblin). This was a 1,000-page state-of-the-art piece of policy wonkery. New York's Democratic Senator Daniel Patrick Moynihan's reaction: "Anyone who thinks [Hillarycare] can work in the real world as presently written isn't living in it."

Then the bill entered the noisy, messy congressional sausage factory. Interest groups (most notably the health insurance companies), the usual conservative-libertarian suspects, and internal congressional politicking bred a plethora of competing plans. Health care reform went into Sleeping-Beautyrest until awakened by Prince Obama.[7]

One final analogue is George W. Bush's Medicare Part D, which added prescriptions to Medicare's subsidized benefits. This was the largest expansion of the nation's health care system since Medicare/Medicaid in the 1960s. It came before a Congress that was Republican, but not overwhelmingly so: the GOP enjoyed margins of thirty-one votes in the House and eleven in the Senate. The proposal was fiercely attacked for its cost and cumbersomeness. But by a whisker-thin (and deviously secured) vote of 220 to 215 (the same one that Speaker Pelosi would get for Obamacare in 2009), Speaker Dennis Hastert and Majority Leader Tom DeLay secured its passage in the House. The Senate easily imposed cloture, and passed it by the same size as the Republicans' eleven-vote majority—though eleven Democrats voted for the bill and nine Republicans voted against it.

As might be expected of a law with a GOP provenance, Bush's prescription bill sought to provide coverage through market mechanisms. There was no overarching government system, but rather some forty private plans which were set loose to compete with one another. To general surprise, it worked better than expected. The Congressional Budget Office initially estimated that the plan would cost $640 billion over its first decade. But as of January 2010, its estimate had shrunk to $410 billion.[8]

■ ■ ■

These analogues offer an instructive history lesson; but like all such, it is subject to varied readings. One is that large legislative changes are best served by an initially modest presentation, in which familiar concepts— insurance, the market, self-sufficiency—are given due regard. So it was with Social Security's introduction, with Medicare, with Bush's prescription plan. More grandiose approaches—Harry Truman's stillborn national insurance scheme, the Clintons' plan—seem to make the same point in a negative way. Obama, understandably, read the record differently: not as a series of object lessons but as a challenge to be met.

He was well aware of the Clintons' mistake in letting a conclave of policy wonks define Hillarycare before the pols got a look-see. All well and good. But the seventy-plus years of social welfare policymaking since Social Security in 1935 taught a different lesson. Even when large congressional majorities (as in 1935 and 1965) and a highly propitious political atmosphere (that of the New Deal and the Great Depression, or of post-1964 and the turbulent 'sixties) are in place—even then, it is wise to make your congressional coalition as broad and deep as possible and to make your legislation as modest and hedged-about as possible.

Political scientist Edward Banfield's caution—"Don't just do something; stand there"—may serve well enough at most times. But sometimes the moment comes for large action, as it did in 1935 and 1965, and perhaps in 2009–2010. But even then it was best not to run, but walk, to the heavenly gates of policy immortality.

The fact that Obamacare is now law might seem to contradict these precepts. But it is clear that its passage was due in large part to its pullbacks on the public option, abortion funding, and taxation: twenty-first century equivalents to Social Security's initial exclusions. And it remains to be seen what will be the consequences of Obamacare's uniquely partisan political origins when, inevitably, the wheel of party supremacy turns.

There were, in retrospect, two interconnected dimensions to the fortunes of Obamacare. One was the web of conflicting interests, aspirations, and ideas that shaped its character: The Devilish Details. The other was its legislative journey—how it was shepherded through Congress on its way to the president's signature: to echo (or distort) Bunyan, The Bill's Grim Progress.

THE DEVILISH DETAILS

It quickly became clear that a bill, as both supporters and opponents endlessly said, affecting between a sixth and a seventh of the American economy would be chockablock with devilish details.

President Obama's approach to health care was determined in good part by his desire to avoid the disaster that befell Hillarycare in 1993, much as the French General Staff long devoted itself to winning the previous war. This led to an initial leave-it-to-the-congressional-leadership approach that fed more than a year of frustration and controversy.

It is not clear who drafted the various versions of health care reform that floated in and out of the media's overview during the spring and summer of 2009. Henry Waxman, chairman of Energy and Commerce, Charles Rangel of Ways and Means, and George Miller of Education and Labor were important House players. And Speaker Nancy Pelosi was a conspicuous voice for the liberal causes of a public option and hefty taxes on the rich.

At critical moments there would be White House interventions, with Budget Director Peter Orszag and White House health care czar Nancy-Ann DeParle much in evidence. Chief of Staff Rahm Emanuel dealt with Congress in his behind-the-scenes Chicago way. And Obama himself brought the Obamacare message (whatever, at the moment, that message might be) to the public as the congressional process dragged along.[9]

It is arguable that the president suffered a serious early loss when former Senate majority leader Tom Daschle, tapped to be his chief health care consultant, had to withdraw because of some dicey financial arrangements. In June 2009 Daschle and Republican Bob Dole proposed a health care compromise. But they were former, not current, senators; and the Bipartisan Policy Center that they founded had, in the current fervid political atmosphere, an almost antique ring to it.[10]

Outgoing Energy and Commerce chair John Dingell introduced America's Affordable Health Choices Act in the House on July 14, 2009. Its 1,017 pages added up to a decades-long liberal health care wish list, much as the Stimulus Act did for other government spending projects.

The bill put a liberal stamp on a wide range of ancillary long-term health care issues. It included a designed-to-grow public option; it accepted a place for abortion in a government-supported system; the costs of the expansion were to be borne by taxing the well-off and bringing in a wonderland of hitherto untapped efficiencies.

The Republicans, who had a long record of unresponsiveness to the health care coverage problem, had their own, less expansive wish list. Unsurprisingly, these had more to do with efficiency and cost-containment than equity and comprehensive coverage. They proposed a limit on the medical malpractice suits beloved of trial lawyers, which did appear to ratchet up doctors' costs; a wide market of competing insurance companies in each state (much like the Medicare D prescription drug system) instead of the more cartel-like arrangements for Medicare; and catastrophic insurance policies as one way to deal with the disparity in health insurance needs that separated the healthy, and often uninsured, young from their illness-plagued elders.

These were ideas worthy of consideration. But they were an ill fit with the Democratic liberal agenda. The leadership (with the assent of Obama, it appears) made no serious effort to include Republicans, or their ideas, in the Obamacare package.[11]

By turning over the bill's details to the House Democratic leaders, Obama sought to escape the wonkery taint that so damaged Hillarycare. In order to avoid the Clintons' Harry-and-Louise problem (influential insurance company-sponsored TV commercials that featured an appealing anti-Hillarycare couple), deals were made with the major players in the health care game.

These included the American Medical Association; the leading drug companies (Big Pharma); the largest health care insurers; and AARP, the self-designated voice of the Medicare generation. Each was brought into the Obamacare tent.

AARP's endorsement was not unconnected to the prospect of rich profits accruing to the organization from the sale of Medicare supplementary insurance. (This despite the growing public belief that Medicare recipients stood to gain little or nothing, and perhaps to lose a good deal, from Obamacare.)

The AMA initially opposed the public option and came under heavy fire from the Left for doing so. But, presumably lured by the prospect of a massive increase in its doctors' patient base and perhaps by the tide of support for Obamacare from mainstream opinion outlets, the AMA was on board by July, when the House bill was introduced.

Even the insurance companies—the favored villains of Congress and the administration during the long march to passage—thought they had a deal of sorts with the powers that be: the lure of bigger profits from expanded enrollment, and little pressure on them to commit to a specific cost-cutting approach.

The diciest deal was with Big Pharma. Billy Tauzin, the companies' chief lobbyist, struck a bargain with White House Chief of Staff Rahm Emanuel which gained the assent of Senate Finance Committee chair Max Baucus and White House health policy honcho Nancy-Ann DeParle. The large pharmaceutical companies agreed to support the bill, public option and all, ditching their one-time co-conspirators, the large health insurance firms. In return, Emanuel and Company pledged to support a notably modest $80 billion cap on the cost savings that Big Pharma was obligated to accrue over the first decade of Obamacare. But Speaker Pelosi quickly made it clear that the House was not bound to that deal: a portent of more and larger clashes of interest to come.[12]

By the traditional measure of the primacy of vested interests in an issue of this scale, Obama might rightly assume that he had his ducks in a row. And it was not unreasonable for him to think that by giving the lead to Congress he had assured the measure's legislative success. Polls showed solid if not overwhelming public support for a large health care reform bill. And the media lived up to its pro-Obama reputation in supporting the legislation.

So why was its passage so drawn-out, contentious, and uncertain? On one level, it can be blamed on strategic decisions by Obama, his staff, Pelosi, and Reid which in retrospect were seriously flawed. That leads to another question: how did they finally get things right enough to emerge with a health care bill?

To try to answer these questions takes us into the culture of the early twenty-first century American polity. It is tempting in this context to fasten on one highly relevant fact of contemporary American life. For all the manifest defects of health insurance in America—of cost, coverage, access—the social reality is that over 80 percent of Americans have some form of health insurance, and over 80 percent of these appear to be more or less satisfied with it. It is true that between 35 and 50 million Americans are uncovered. And in its broadest reach, Obamacare proposes to embrace 94 percent of the population. Starting from ground zero (as, in their ways, Social Security and Medicare did), this would be the wondrous social achievement that supporters claim it to be. Starting from 80-plus percent, it can be regarded as a relatively incremental social gain.

▪ ▪ ▪

The mechanics of the bill were so complex, and the details so technical and so obscured by the measure's length, that there was relatively little public discussion of its nuts and bolts. Debate focused, rather, on the extraordinary number of controversial policy issues that Obamacare raised.

The public option—the inclusion of a separate government-run insurance alternative—became the focal point for the more ideologically minded liberal and conservative tails of the public opinion bell curve. Health Care for America NOW! and Moveon.org, as well as some of the larger public service unions (which had a practical interest in the expanded public workforce required to oversee Obamacare), put millions of their dollars as well as their PR mouths behind the public option cause.

But a senior White House adviser confessed: "I don't understand why the Left of the Left has decided that this is their Waterloo. . . . I don't understand how [the public option] . . . has become the measure of whether what we achieve is health care reform." Harvard health care guru David Cutler called the public option "this unholy grail."

Although it was by no means clear that the inclusion of the public option would lead to a government-run health care system, liberals looked forward expectantly, and conservatives looked forward apprehensively, to that outcome. Just as its advocates called for a "robust public option," supporters of a private system sought a "robust individual mandate." One scary—or hopeful—estimate was that under the House health care bill as many as 88 million employees would shift—or be shifted—from employer plans to a public system. In unguarded moments, Congressman Barney Frank and Speaker Pelosi gave vent to their expectation that a "single-payer system" (the Left-liberal euphemism of choice; its right-wing equivalent is "socialized medicine") would morph from a foot in the door to an 800-pound gorilla in the room.

Obama sought to put a softer face on things when he equated the public option's likely impact on private health insurance with the supposedly bracing competitive effect of the Postal Service on UPS and FedEx. His analogy was rendered less effective by the widespread view that, as Obama himself conceded, "It's the Post Office that's always having problems."

The issue did not galvanize the bulk of the citizenry. Depending on how the public option was perceived—as one of a variety of competitive forms of coverage; as a last, Medicaid-like resort for those unable to afford regular health insurance; or as a tax-subsidized alternative to private insurance—poll opinions ranged from strongly favorable to mildly unfavorable.

Why did the public option bite the dust in the Senate bill? On the face of it, Connecticut's Joe Lieberman, in his persona as the necessary sixtieth vote to impose cloture and get the bill passed, secured its elimination. But early on, Obama sent signals that this wasn't a make-or-break part of the bill. In the event, Obama, Reid, and Pelosi readily scuttled the public option when it became too big an obstacle to the passage of health care reform. Their doing so was testimony to the fact that when ideology, however heartfelt, came up against the facts of American political life, principle was likely to give way to interest.[13]

▪ ▪ ▪

Less contentious was the cause of bringing as many as possible of the substantial number of uninsured Americans into the health care system. Estimates of the number varied widely, from 30 million to 50 million. No more precise was the perception of the makeup of this group. Each year something like 20 million people went through an uninsured period in the course of changing jobs. About 40 percent of the uninsured in Florida, California, Texas, New Mexico, and Arizona were immigrants; and 21 percent of those uncovered were illegal immigrants, who raised a separate eligibility issue.

Some 14 million people were eligible for existing programs such as Medicare and Medicaid, but for a variety of reasons did not participate. Among the uninsured, 9 million to 10 million had incomes of $75,000 or more, which should have made insurance affordable for them. And one in three Americans between the ages of twenty and twenty-nine—about 13 million individuals—saw no need for health insurance: what might be called the Fountain of Youth syndrome.

Like Social Security and Medicare, a comprehensive national health care system needed the fullest possible participation. To induce, or compel, those outside to join was a constant and not readily resolved dilemma. As Obamacare evolved, sticks (fines and even jail terms) won favor over carrots (differential coverage and premiums).[14]

How to deal with so complex and varied a mix? There was general agreement on a Medicare-like system without its age limit as the most expeditious way to bring universality to health care. But this raised the issue that came to dominate the debate: what would be the costs of reform, how would they be met, and how could they be reduced?

Should costs and benefits be universal, or should they be pegged to age, condition, income? Which was the proper model: one-size-fits-all Social Security and Medicare, or custom-tailored automobile insurance? Could so vast a change be accomplished without new taxes save on the very rich, and with long-term savings from efficiency, as Obama wanted? Or was it better to end the tax exclusion of employer-sponsored plans, a World War II survivor, as John McCain proposed in the 2008 campaign and Obama roundly rejected? The tension between the demands of affordability on the one hand and the need for accessibility on the other became a major source of contention as the debate wore on.

It seemed initially that the Democratic proffer of greater access and coverage with no increase in cost was likely to carry the day. Blue Dog Democrat Jim Cooper of Tennessee observed, "It's a lot easier to be Santa than Scrooge." But matters of concern—some long-present, others fresh on the scene—multiplied.

One provision of the House bill was the creation of health insurance exchanges, the Democrats' alternative to the GOP idea of an interstate market of competing insurance companies. Another Republican cause, a cap on malpractice tort liability awards, met with little favor in a Democratic party obligated to generous-donor trial lawyers.

The House bill provided for an Independent Medical Advisory Council (IMAC) to decide on issues of cost, quality, the "applicable conditions" for hospital readmissions, and the like. This brewed up a storm of disapprobation. Conservative critics such as former Alaska Governor Sarah Palin spoke expansively of "death panels" deciding on matters of life (and death) for patients. Critics pointed out that these decisions were not subject to bureaucratic or judicial review.

They were unhappy, too, with provisions that gave uncontained power to the secretary of health and human services to adjust payments deemed excessive or deficient, and that made a package of routine coverage and catastrophic insurance illegal under the bill's standard of "acceptable coverage." And complaints arose over the requirement that small businesses had to provide the federal standard of insurance or pay an 8 percent payroll tax. The conspiracy-minded saw in this yet another device to induce private insurance providers to give up the ghost and turn things over to a government program.[15]

These were nuts-and-bolts issues, presumably open to legislative deal-making. But without anyone much expecting it, abortion became a potentially deal-busting issue. As many as forty Democratic members of Congress with pro-life constituencies and/or strong personal beliefs were reluctant to go along with Obamacare unless the House bill had a forceful disclaimer of the use of government money for abortions.

Pelosi accepted an amendment that did precisely that, perhaps on the assumption that the ultimate House-Senate bill would backtrack. In the event, enough anti-abortion Democrats voted for the House bill to assure its five-vote passage. Public funding of abortion in the House, like the public option in the Senate, was a casualty of the political truism that the larger your majority and the more ambitious your legislative goal, the more complex and substantial are the obstacles that arise.[16]

Other concerns remained, or kept cropping up, to endanger support for Obamacare. A substantial tax on high-end health insurance plans was an attractive source of revenue to help pay for the additional cost of greatly expanded coverage. Obama chose to speak of plans that belonged to investment bankers and other favored beings. But union leaders focused on such insurance held by their members.[17]

The established congressional practice of yearly fixes to top off doctors' Medicare compensation became enmeshed in the growing concern over the cost of Obamacare. A Senate proposal to offload onto the deficit an estimated $250 billion of these costs in the first decade of Obamacare was opposed by twelve Senate Democrats as well as all Republicans: a nice instance of the difficulty of keeping your legislative ducks in a row when the issue is as fecund with difficulties as this one was.

Relatively little discussed, for reasons that are not quite clear, was the need to provide for the substantial increase in doctors, nurses, and the other medical personnel and infrastructure required to deal with an additional 30 million or more insured patients. As the situation of Medicaid suggested, access was an uncertain entitlement if health care providers weren't available.

While the AMA backed Obamacare, other members of the medical establishment did not. The deans of the Harvard and Johns Hopkins medical schools had substantial reservations. The Mayo Clinic announced that it would not continue to serve Medicare patients. From another quarter, Libertarian John Mackey, the CEO of Whole Foods, wanted less government control, more insurance company competition, high-deductible health insurance plans, and health savings accounts. He thereby enraged the more collectivist-minded members of his dietetically correct chain's clientele.[18]

Another sleeper issue suddenly awoke. Between 15 million and 20 million new participants—half of the total—would have to rely on Medicaid. Under existing rules the states had to pick up a substantial part of the bill. How much? California Governor Arnold Schwarzenegger estimated that it would cost his state $8 billion a year. Reliably liberal Wisconsin Senator Russ Feingold refused to support a law that so additionally burdened states and counties.[19]

THE BILL'S GRIM PROGRESS

After the 1,017-page health care bill was introduced in mid-July 2009, Speaker Pelosi hoped to see it pass the House in time for the August recess. By the traditional rules of bill-making, it seemed that Obama and the congressional leadership had things pretty well in hand. Polls showed general public support; the media were supportive; the big interest groups were in tow; the party had solid congressional majorities.

But as things played out, a very different dynamic emerged. At this point it is not possible to determine the relative responsibility of mismanagement, the inherent complexity of the issue, and the political culture of the early twenty-first century for what ensued. But all are worth our attention.

The process was not simplified by the facts that three House committees initially endorsed bills. These were melded into the one introduced in July. Two Senate committees were poised to sink their teeth into whatever was passed by the lower chamber.

The inescapable intricacies of congressional bill-making sufficiently explain why Pelosi was unable to meet her pre-August-recess goal of House passage. But something new and unexpected emerged when House members went home for their summertime break. Ugly confrontations broke out at town meetings. Pelosi and others on the Left spoke darkly of the whiff of fascism. A fairer estimate would be that these outbursts were in the tradition of direct political protest that emerged during the anti-Vietnam 1960s: teach-ins, so to speak, without a campus gloss.

In retrospect we can see that the town hall meetings, and the Tea Party movement that in part came out of it, marked the political emergence of a conservative populism. Spurred by such benchmarks as the November elections in Virginia and New Jersey and the January election in Massachusetts, this was arguably the most dynamic new political force to emerge thus far in the Obama presidency.

Its most immediate sources were the concerns stoked by the likely cost and broad sweep of Obamacare. These were coupled with, and energized by, the view that the first order of government business was the economy, as well as widespread unhappiness with the bank bailouts, mounting government debt, and, most of all, the high level of unemployment.

The affluent liberal/progressive wing of the Democratic party, relatively sheltered from the recession's impact, remained predisposed to focus on the more ideologically fulfilling issue of health care. But those inclined to the liberal persuasion were not growing in number. The rigors of the recession and the scale of government spending appeared to be turning liberals into that most cuddly of causes, an endangered species. A late October 2009 poll found citizens who leaned in a conservative direction to be growing in number; those who identified themselves as liberal remained at their customary 20 percent.[20]

By the summer's end, much of the initial impetus for the bill's passage appeared to have dissipated. Obama spoke constantly on the issue, including a much-hyped September appearance before a joint session of Congress. (Clinton tried the same ploy for *his* health care bill in September 1993, to no effect.)

But Obama took a much more removed stance when it came to legislative specifics. In July his rhetoric subtly shifted from reforming the health care *system* to reforming health care *insurance*: recognition of the lack of popular support for root-and-branch change and the prospect of tapping popular support for populist insurance-company bashing.[21]

Did he hurt or help his cause by this strategy? The long months of fractious debate, and the public and political hard feelings that came with passage, are arguments against it. But his ultimate success argues more persuasively in its favor. Pundit Norman Ornstein, a liberal outlier in the conservative American Enterprise

Institute, thought in September that the legislative process was functioning in a normal way and that Obama showed considerable political realism by avoiding specific commitments and relying on congressional party leaders. Presciently, he expected Obama to intervene more forcefully in the final stage and predicted that a substantial bill would be passed.[22]

The lack of clear momentum spurred efforts to reach out to at least some members of the other party. Former Democratic Senator Bill Bradley suggested that Republicans, and their medical malpractice and expanded insurance exchange proposals, should be more visible parts of the health care reform effort. But aside from Senate Finance Committee Chairman Max Baucus, the congressional leadership (and for that matter Obama) showed little or no interest in wooing a few Republicans by seriously considering some GOP proposals. Nor did Republicans show any particular desire to participate. Shaky popular support for the bill and a polarized political culture saw to that.[23]

■ ■ ■

The process came to a head in late 2009 and early 2010. At the end of October, Pelosi finally unveiled a composite of three House committee bills crafted during the summer. Stretching for almost 2,000 pages, costing a trillion dollars over ten years, complete with a public option and hearty taxes on the rich, the bill epitomized the liberal health care vision and presumably reflected Obama's true desires. Pelosi set the bill in a grand historical context: "We come before you to follow in the footsteps of those who gave our country Social Security and then Medicare."

But opposition inexorably grew. Blue Dog moderates were troubled by the cost of the proposal. And a number of them began to criticize the lack of a provision to ban the use of government funds for abortions. Employers objected to the tax increases proposed to pay for the reform. Doctors were troubled by unclear reimbursement provisions, health insurers by cost constraints.[24]

Democrats didn't help much, splitting into those who wanted the bill rejected as inadequate (Howard Dean, Daily Kos, etc.) and "realists" such as Senator Bob Casey of Pennsylvania ("Any big agreement is progress, even if we do not know any of the details."). When Pelosi agreed to compromises such as a stiff no-funding-for-abortion provision, progressives got antsy. Progressive Caucus head Lynn Woolsey declared: "No way we're voting for a bill that's got this stuff in it."[25]

But Pelosi's compromises turned out to be necessary. The House approved the bill in November by a five-vote margin, with only one Republican in favor. More significant: thirty-nine Democrats—half of the party's House majority—opposed it.

Obama's decision to turn matters over to Congress may have avoided the ruffled legislative feathers that the Clintons stirred up. But it had its own built-in difficulties. In the Senate Finance Committee, Montana's Max Baucus took charge of drafting a bill. He had a constituency, and hence an approach to health care, quite different from those of San Francisco liberal Pelosi or Los Angeles liberal Henry Waxman.

In order to put a patina of bipartisanship on health care reform, and assure cloture and hence no Republican filibuster, Baucus convened a bipartisan "gang of six" committee members (skipping staunch liberals such as Jay Rockefeller, Charles Schumer, and John Kerry) to thrash out a plan acceptable to a few Republicans. Discussions went on for months, with the holy grail of sixty assured votes tantalizingly close. But there was a persistent inability to come to agreement on hot-button issues such as the public option and abortion.

Baucus finally sent a bill to the Senate floor in October, where Majority Leader Reid took charge as Pelosi had since July in the House. Pressure to come up with a more moderate version than the House bill was intense; the influence of senators from the less blue states was much greater than that of their counterparts in the House.

Reid's readiness to make deals put Pelosi to shame. He finally secured the sixty votes he needed to invoke cloture at the very end of December, with a bill sagging like an overdressed Christmas tree with treats aimed at particular senators. In some ways, it was reminiscent of tariff-making in past days: in particular, the Smoot-Hawley Tariff Act of 1930, when the old balance of protection and free trade interests collapsed under the strain of the gathering Depression. Social Security and Medicare were hardly immaculate conceptions. But the Cornhusker Compromise, the Louisiana Purchase, and a clutch of other special provisions (not exempting Reid's own Nevada) attracted much adverse attention and further clouded the policy case for Obamacare.[26]

Polls in early 2010 revealed that popular support was continuing to erode. The cause was not helped by the unexpected election of Republican Scott Brown to Ted Kennedy's seat for Massachusetts, in part on the basis of his opposition to Obamacare.

The prospect for health care reform darkened further in January 2010 when the Senate's version went to the House. The customary House-Senate negotiation to come up with a mutually acceptable single bill was not in the cards after Brown deprived the Democrats of their cloture-invoking sixty-vote Senate majority.

In response, the House leadership turned to the reconciliation process, never before used for a bill of this magnitude. That meant that the House had to pass the Senate bill as it was, and channel its modifications into a separate amending statute.

What ensued was a disconcerting reprise of the Senate orgy of special-interest sops. In closed sessions that discarded reiterated commitments to openness, the leaders set a new standard of questionable understandings secretly arrived at.

Such doings were hardly unknown before: the Tom DeLay years come readily to mind. But there was a discomfiting disconnect between the moral stance of the Obama presidency and the Pelosi House. Among the jewels in this tarnished crown: union, but not non-union, workers would for some years be free of a tax levied on high-benefit ("Cadillac") plans. And if push came to shove, the leadership said it would use the obscure "self-executing rule"—"deem and pass" in common parlance—that would enable the House to "pass" the Senate bill without actually voting on it.[27]

Then came the March Miracle: House passage of the Senate bill, the president signing it into law, and almost unqualified Senate acceptance of the House's reconciliation amendments, also signed into law, which together stand as the enactment of Obamacare. What had seemed a lost cause became a found one.

Obama signed the health care bill on March 23, 2010. Eight months had passed since Dingell introduced the first version on July 14, 2009: about as long as it took to pass Social Security, though twice the time it took to pass Medicare.

THE SHAPE AND SOURCES OF SUCCESS

A solid majority for one party is not in itself a guarantee of an easy ride to legislative success. At a time of high autonomy for individual legislators and weakened party discipline (though strengthened ideological division), the correlation between majority size and ease of legislative enactment is weak.

Indeed, the larger the party majority, the more numerous the members from shaky districts not necessarily in sympathy with the party's policies. The Democrats' triumphs in 2006 and 2008 added substantially to the number who represented constituencies that normally leaned Republican. Yet the political dynamic of our time, enhanced by the lack of get-along-by-going-along bosses and machines and by the ideological leanings of the media, advocacy groups, and the blogosphere, favor the ideological antipodes over the moderate middle ground.[28]

Until recently, successful legislation tended to attract or even rely on interparty majorities. These could be sweeping: Social Security, Civil Rights, Voting Rights, Medicare, No Child Left Behind. Or they could be strongly contested and depend on support across party lines: NAFTA, Clinton's welfare reform. Or—increasingly so— they could be almost entirely reliant on the incumbent party: Bush's tax cuts and Medicare D prescription drugs bills; Obama's economic stimulus and health care bills.

The historical trend is clear and is vivid testimony to the polarization of recent politics. Obamacare passed with *no* member of the opposition party supporting the measure: unique in the modern history of important social legislation. (See table of Votes on Major Legislation, 1935–2010 on page 100.)

■ ■ ■

Three factors appear to have been determinative in health care's ultimate passage: Obama's more forceful interventionist role; Pelosi's persuasive skills (in both the Socratic and *Godfather* senses); and contingent external events, most conspicuously a sudden hike in premium rates by some of the big insurance companies.

The most obvious new element was the change in the character of Obama's intercession. In both the specifics

Votes on Major Legislation, 1935–2010

Legislation		House		Senate	
		For	Against	For	Against
Social Security	D	284	15	60	1
(1935)	R	81	15	16	5
Civil Rights	D	153	91	46	21
(1964)	R	136	35	27	6
Voting Rights	D	221	61	47	17
(1965)	R	112	24	30	2
Medicare	D	137	48	57	7
(1965)	R	70	68	13	17
NAFTA	D	102	156	27	27
(1993)	R	132	47	34	10
Welfare Reform	D	98	97	25	21
(1996)	R	230	2	53	0
No Child Left	D	197	10	41	6
Behind (2001)	R	186	34	46	3
Medicare D	D	16	189	11	35
(2003)	R	204	25	42	9
Tax Cuts	D	10	198	12	31
(2004)	R	224	0	46	2
Stimulus	D	244	11	61	0
(2009)	R	0	176	3	37
Health Care	D	219	34	60	0
(2010)	R	0	178	0	39
Financial Reform	D	223	0	57	1
(2010)	R	0	176	3	38

of what finally emerged and in the mechanics of the push for final passage, one can see a reprise of the talents that won him his nomination and election.

Obama's speechifying—his chief contribution to the health care reform enterprise to this point—continued and even intensified. But he became less professorial, less content to lecture polite but not highly energized audiences. And in the LBJ tradition, he turned to the carrot-and-stick persuasion of reachable members of Congress.

He dealt with the Republicans in ways that lessened the perception (although perhaps not the reality) that he was unresponsive to their ideas. He met in televised sessions with House Republicans in Baltimore on January 29 and led a bipartisan Blair House summit on February 25. This was favorable turf. His communication skills and command of the issue may not have placated a doubtful public or wooed Republicans. But it appears to have reassured skittish House Democrats.

Most of all, Obama came out on March 3 with his own proposal: essentially the Senate bill, with a few minor sops to Republican ideas. He tempered some of the less reputable appendages of the Senate and House bills—Nebraska's exemption from additional state Medicaid payments, union members' exemptions from a tax on their "Cadillac" health plans—with that most effective of emollients, money: he made these favors universal. Creative accounting kept the cost of his bill to $950 billion, between the Senate measure's $872 billion and the House's mantra-breaking trillion.[29]

Liberal-Left Democrats were generally acquiescent with legislation that dropped the public option and assured right-to-lifers that no federal funds would be used for abortions. Why? One hint came in a remark that Obama is supposed to have made to congressional liberals: "This is a foundation. Thirty-one million Americans will be covered under this. It's a beginning."

What did he mean by this? Presumably something more than that the remaining 10 million to 20 million uncovered Americans—5 percent to 10 percent of the population—would be included later. Rather it reflects and illuminates the thrust of the "New Foundation" label that he sought initially (with indifferent success) to attach to his legislative program. His "beginning," it is safe to assume, refers to the first step on a journey to a universal system of government-provided health care.[30]

Obama intertwined two conflicting themes: this was the greatest expansion of social policy since Medicare (or Social Security); and it would have little or no impact on Americans who did not wish to change their existing health care coverage. (In this he echoed Mr. Dooley's summation of Theodore Roosevelt on the trusts: "On wan hand I wud stamp thim undher foot; on th' other hand not so fast.")

This perhaps explains the tenacity with which Obama insisted on the not readily obvious linkage of massive growth in health care and massive savings in costs, and his seeming disregard of the numerous red lights emanating from public opinion. It explains also his disinterest (aside from occasional lip service) in the woo-some-Republicans option.[31]

History's judgment may be that the passage of Obamacare confirms that the modern presidency is a bully pulpit indeed. A previous, though lesser, analogue was the ability of George W. Bush to secure his Medicare prescription plan in the face of much congressional hostility.

■ ■ ■

As the health care debate entered its final stage, most expert, and not-so-expert, opinion doubted that Pelosi would be able to put together a House majority that (as the terms of the reconciliation process dictated) would accept the Senate bill as is.[32]

But Pelosi's toughness—a mix of San Francisco liberal ideological certitude and a Baltimore-born take-no-prisoners leadership style—turned out to be of considerable consequence. She may not be, as one idolater put it, the most powerful woman in history. But she did display a Margaret Thatcher-like tenacity, supposedly bucking up Obama to stay the course and not accept a lesser compromise, in the spirit of Thatcher's admonition to the elder Bush: "Don't go all wobbly on me, George."

And finally there was the ever-present but never predictable element of contingency. Several insurance companies made the ill-judged decision to substantially raise their premiums at the height of the Obama-Pelosi effort to reverse the tide of public opinion. At the very least it burnished the argument that Obamacare addressed a real problem.

OBAMACARE IN HISTORY

There is an incontestable need for more inclusive, and less costly, health care. Obamacare does much to meet the first goal. But it is by no means clear that it responds to the second (and arguably more pressing) concern.

From the first, there was a disconnect between the elevated vision of Obama and his supporters of what a comprehensive health care system might be, and the grubby American reality of a dense web of existing interests, beliefs, and expectations. There is much to the observation of a conservative critic: "The health care bill is big, complex, incomprehensible and coercive—all the things people hate nowadays."[33]

The chattering classes Left and Right are united in the view that this is legislation of portentous magnitude. Its advocates claim that Obamacare is the most important social measure since Medicare and will usher in a new era of broad, assured coverage and large-scale cost savings. Against this utopia is the dystopia of conservative critics, who see it as a hodgepodge of intrusive mandates, clunky regulation, and disastrously large spending. *Their* new era is one of socialism and bankruptcy.

Both visions, it can be argued, are overblown. It is far from certain that Obamacare will take an iconic place beside Social Security and Medicare. There are questions of constitutionality (though the likelihood of a successful challenge is doubtful), an implementation timetable that stretches for years, and no sign as yet of the broad support that made Social Security and Medicare political untouchables.

One big difference is that those predecessors broke fresh ground. Unemployment compensation and old age pensions were rare birds indeed in 1935. So was comprehensive medical insurance for over-65ers in 1965. But Obamacare takes effect in a society where more than 80 percent of eligible individuals have health care insurance and are reasonably satisfied with what they have. The group most likely to benefit from Obamacare is the 30 million-plus uninsured. This is a substantial number. But they make up only about 10 percent of the American population.

Other potential beneficiaries are those rejected for insurance due to poor health or dropped from the insurance rolls. Precise figures as to their size are elusive. One of the nurses' unions estimated that over 20 percent of insurance applicants are denied coverage. Another estimate is that from 2004 to 2007, 12.6 million people were rejected. But this covers all denials, for whatever reason. The companies claim that only about 2 percent of "clear claims" (without non-medical problems) are rejected.

Rescission—removal of coverage—is also a subject of debate. One claim is that about 20,000 policyholders in three large companies had their coverage removed over a five-year period. A problem to be addressed, surely. But by an overhaul of the entire system?

The number of Medicaid recipients—43.5 million in 2008—will expand exponentially. But provisions to shield the states from the much larger costs this will impose are far from in place. Nor is it clear how Medicaid recipients will be able to avoid more crowded, or less available, doctor care or hospital services.[34]

Of the 80 percent-plus currently covered, few are likely to benefit from Obamacare and many are likely to be harmed by higher costs and lesser services. More than 200 million people, nearly 70 percent of the population, have either employer-provided or private insurance plans. Add the nearly 45 million Medicare recipients as of 2008, and five-sixths of the population has coverage that is unlikely to be improved, and quite possibly may be harmed, by Obamacare.

And then there are its dicey economics. The likelihood that Obamacare will stay within its predicted fiscal parameters is lessened both by past precedent and by the plan's own terms. Never has a large entitlement program stayed anywhere close to its projected budgetary bounds. Removing the "doctor fix" that Congress regularly passes to supplement physicians' Medicare reimbursements does not inspire confidence. Nor does double-counting Social Security income, or applying a decade of Obamacare revenue to six years of expenditure, or putting cost-cutting in the hands of a toothless Independent Payment Advisory Board.[35]

The political significance of Obamacare is no less clouded. There are no strong historical grounds for believing that Obama will stand or fall on health care reform. Clinton's presidency did not collapse because of the failure of Hillarycare; Lyndon Johnson's presidency was not saved by the success of Medicare. Conservative conventional wisdom regards Carter's presidency as a failed one; liberal conventional wisdom does the same for Bush. Yet in neither case was major legislation at fault, but rather failed or widely unpopular executive actions: in Carter's case, the Iranian hostage crisis; in Bush's case, the Iraq war.

Nor is Obamacare certain to affect the fall 2010 congressional elections, adversely or favorably. The historical precedent of the incumbent party losing ground, the continued weight of unemployment, and the impressive capacity of the Republicans to alienate popular opinion can be at least as determining.[36]

▪ ▪ ▪

In retrospect, Obama and the congressional leadership might have been well advised to heed history's object lesson and conclude that wisdom and prudence dictated a serious attempt to mediate between the ideological purity of the Democratic base and the desirability of respectable Republican participation in so sweeping a reform.

The major Republican proposals would not have seriously changed the rather amorphous, and almost certainly more expensive than predicted, package that ultimately emerged. True, Republican leaders were no more inclined to cooperate with the Democrats on health care than Democratic leaders were inclined to seek bipartisanship (except on their own terms). But it was likely that some Republican votes could have been garnered if a serious effort at compromise had been undertaken.

Quite possibly (as a couple of moderate Democratic pros argue), less would have had to be compromised away if the legislative effort had not been so polarized. And surely the future of Obamacare would be more secure if it had come into being with something like the general political and public acceptance of its Social Security and Medicare predecessors.[37]

It is clear by now that Obama is driven more than most presidents by the conviction that he is in office to do great things, and that this conviction is embedded in a more strongly social democratic world view than any chief executive since FDR. Health care came closer than his other major causes—job creation, finance reform, immigration reform, energy and climate control—to fulfilling those aspirations and beliefs. But whether it will take hold in American public policy as Social Security and Medicare did, or run into dense and growing public disaffection, has yet to be seen.

Contexts: Analogy and Ideology

AS HIS FIRST TERM APPROACHES its mid-point, there is a widespread perception that Obama has not lived up to his initial promise. In truth, his record isn't all that slight, and the passage of health care reform in March 2010 and financial reform in July add substantially to it. The problem lies rather in the high expectations that Obama engendered among the chattering classes, the widespread belief in the incompetence and misdirection of the Bush administration combined with the sense that Obama isn't altering things all that much, and the lack of signs that he is broadening, or even sustaining, his base of popular support.

Perhaps the most striking aspect of Obama's performance so far is neither the gestures to the Left that many conservatives bemoan, or the concessions to the middle way that many progressives bewail. Rather, his administration is most notable for its *ordinariness*: for falling prey to all too familiar misjudgments as to political power, policy choices and their consequences, public attitudes and opinion. These missteps are the common lot of American presidents, but were thought to be less likely in this Regime of All the Talents. The unbearable heaviness of governing, it appears, falls with majestic impartiality on whoever occupies the presidency.[1]

How do we go about getting a fix on so elusive a president, with so equivocal a record? I've taken a historian's-eye look at three of the more substantive aspects of his administration: his style of governance, his economic initiatives, and Obamacare. Now let's raise our sights a bit higher and wider, and see what can be said at this point about Obama's place in the larger context of the modern American presidency. To what extent has he functioned within, or sought to alter, the prevailing political culture? I will end with some guarded speculation as to the future policy and political prospects of his administration.

THE USES OF ANALOGY

As noted before, so distinctive a president as Obama attracts an unusually large flow of analogy with his predecessors. To some degree this feast of comparison has stood in the stead of attempts to define Obama's presidency in more self-referential terms, as was the case with FDR and LBJ (or, for that matter, Eisenhower, Reagan, and the Bushes). At the same time there has been strikingly little discussion of the meaning and implications of his chosen theme of the New Foundation, in vivid contrast to FDR's New Deal and LBJ's Great Society. In the course of 2009 and the first half of 2010, the *New York Times* and the *Washington Post* linked "Obama" and "New Foundation" only forty-two times.

It is a truism to say of Obama's predecessor George W. Bush that, for better or worse, what you saw was what you got. With the easy arrogance of his breed, progressive columnist Frank Rich observed that while Obama has been equated with historical figures ranging from Roosevelt and Reagan to Kennedy and Adlai Stevenson and even to Hitler and Stalin, it was "amusing" that George Bush analogies tended to be restricted to his parents and Hitler.[2]

While the inclination to match up Obama with his predecessors continues, the favored subjects of comparison have changed. References to FDR's Hundred Days and New Deal and LBJ's Great Society are out of favor. There is no clear consensus on the character or content of Obama's presidential leadership or on where he fits in the prevailing classification of America's chief executives.[3]

This is due in part to his style of communication: Clintonian in volume, alternatively professorial in eloquence and sophistication or grubbily partisan in take-no-prisoners overstatement. The result may be, again, that what you see is what you get; but what do you see? Was French President Nicolas Sarkozy on target when he asked his advisers: *"est-il faible?"* (Is he weak?) Or is Obama at heart the equivalent of French Prime Minister Georges Clemenceau's reputed summation of Woodrow Wilson as someone who talks like Jesus Christ and acts like Lloyd George. Or do the eulogisms of his followers reflect what, in fact, he is?[4]

As the Obama term progressed, the FDR/Hundred Days analogies thick on the ground in the early months gave way to a different model: not a president taking charge in a time of historic policy change, but a president increasingly burdened by the weight of governance.

This progress (or descent) reflects the diminishing expectations attached to the Obama administration. And it makes it highly likely that how Obama will adapt his ambitiously Big Government program to widespread public skepticism, and respond to the darkening political prospects of the 2010 election, will dominate public discourse for the foreseeable future.

By some margin, linkages of Obama's name with that of Bill Clinton have been the most frequent in the course of his presidency. This may reflect not much more than the fact that Clinton was the previous Democratic president, and in retrospect is regarded as a successful one; is still (along with his wife) very much in the public eye; and doesn't overtax the media's limited historical perspective.

Analogies with Jimmy Carter are fewer, but make more sense. Both Carter and Obama came to the presidency all but out of nowhere: a brief stint in the Georgia state senate and a two-year term as governor were of a piece with a brief stint in the Illinois state senate and a truncated term as U.S. senator. Both ran campaigns that battened on widespread distaste for the presidential leadership that preceded them: Nixon-Ford; Bush II. And both spoke appealingly of rising above partisanship and restoring honesty, competence, national unity, and self-confidence to American public life.

Carter and Obama began their terms in office with full agendas of issues and programs: the accumulated wish list of post-1960s liberalism in Carter's case, the agenda of post-1990s liberalism in Obama's case. (It is notable how much overlap there is: health care, energy, the economy, a new and softer approach in foreign policy.) And both ran into unexpected political turbulence in their first year in office.

A conservative predicting what Obama's new presidency would look like saw his election in 2008 not as an echo of FDR's in 1932 or LBJ's in 1964 but of Carter's in 1976. He foresaw no replay of the New Deal or the Great Society: "In three or four years, the main political fact in this country could well be a ruinous crisis of Democratic liberalism."[5]

It is accepted that Carter's response to adversity was to hunker down: to stick to his policy guns in the face of mounting evidence that they were of diminishing political effectiveness and, in consequence, to consign himself to a one-term presidency. Bill Clinton's mid-course correction after the disastrous 1994 by-election is a frequently cited alternative model for Obama to follow. His was a classic instance of political adaptability, with a dramatically different political result: a solid second-term victory and considerably higher standing than Carter in the presidential pecking order.[6]

No one would claim that Clinton had anything like the larger programmatic goals of FDR or LBJ, to which Obama has given considerable rhetorical obeisance. Is Obama capable of echoing Clinton's striking refusal to be a slave to the hobgoblin of consistency? Or is he more likely to adhere to a Carterian commitment to principle, however politically unpromising? Or—and in the wake of the passage of Obamacare and financial reform, this has new standing as a possibility—will he persevere but, unlike Carter, retrieve the popularity and élan of his administration's creation?

Less frequent because they are more remote (but perhaps more germane) are linkages of Obama with Woodrow Wilson, the first Democratic president of the twentieth century, and Ronald Reagan, the most transformative Republican chief executive in recent times. Here the model changes: less the enactment of a legislative program, more the articulation of basic political beliefs about government and society; a policy more than an agenda presidency.[7]

Equations with Reagan are, admittedly, a stretch (though Reagan, like Obama, was seen as detached, "more spectator than leader.") Wilson makes more sense. Obama appears to have a full helping of Wilson's self-assurance, didacticism, and belief in a moral mission. In late 2007 he set forth a declaration of his larger political goals that can only be described as Wilsonian:

"A nation healed. A world repaired. An America that believes again." No less evocative was his observation after he became president: "I am well aware of the expectations that accompany my presidency around the world."

Like Obama, Wilson had early domestic policy successes. But the flow of events and the primacy of the president's role as commander-in-chief drew him into the role of war leader and would-be architect of world peace: a role that ultimately consumed him personally and politically.

Obama has not been reluctant to turn his moralizing style to the tempting if treacherous realm of foreign affairs. This is a path that presidents frustrated by the hazards and ill fortunes of domestic politics are inclined to follow. Think of FDR and World War II, LBJ and Vietnam, George W. Bush and the war on terror.[8]

THE STRUCTURE OF POLITICS IN THE AGE OF OBAMA

But comparisons with predecessors, however illuminating, go only so far in casting light on the causes of presidential policies. It is necessary as well to see Obama's actions in the context of the larger political culture to which he belongs.

Why is a president of whom so much was expected, and who came into office with the most favorable legislative and media environments in decades, not doing better? (It must be said that many of his supporters in the realms of media punditry, academic think-tankery, and left-liberal true-believerism are confident that he has accomplished far more than is generally credited to him. I take this as confirmation that love is indeed blind.)

Obama's communications skills and intelligence understandably continue to be admired by most of the chattering classes and much (though a shrinking much) of the public. And the scope of his ambition to oversee systemic change—in the economy, health care, energy policy, education, foreign policy—remains undimmed in the face of the battering that his agenda has undergone in the course of its first year and more.

Much of this seems inevitable in retrospect, and is by no means Obama's fault. It is no small matter to satisfy a constituency which ranges from volatile college students and affluent members of the liberal Left to African-Americans and skeptical centrists.

The question remains: how will Obama adapt to the altered, decreasingly sympathetic political atmosphere that surrounds him? Even FDR, in the far more attention-focusing circumstances of the Great Depression, had to make major course corrections in policy. He soon distinguished between the immediate need to do something—anything—to relieve the most searing immediate consequences of the Depression and the longer-term social and economic policy changes that recovery and reform appeared to require. This is a distinction that Obama has not so far chosen to make. But then he is confronted by a far less malign national condition.[9]

Lyndon Johnson, second to none in his mastery of the machinery of American government, ran aground on Vietnam and the negative effects of the Great Society: this less than four years after he won one of the great electoral victories in American political history. Obama has not yet had to deal with so consequential a foreign policy setback. But there are signs of a similar disconnect between the strongly social democratic thrust of his domestic initiatives and the predominant mindset of the American people: a potential replay of the reaction against Johnson's War on Poverty.

Yet Obama remains one of the most interesting, intelligent, and original politicians of recent times. It is proper to conclude that his difficulties stem from the larger political milieu as much as from personal mistakes and drawbacks.

The origins of the political culture in which he has to make his way lie in the FDR-New Deal years of the 1930s. But it assumed its current form from the 1960s on. Its most notable features are the decline of political parties as prime dispensers of patronage and power, and the rise of polarized groups on the tails of the political opinion bell curve. Of ever-increasing importance is an "independent" middle, susceptible to the siren call of either party depending on the social-economic or foreign policy situation and political mood of the time.

The decline of party and the increase in both polarization and independence are closely interrelated. The decay of the traditional parties was fostered by the erosion of the regional, ethno-cultural, and class alignments that for more than a century defined them. The same cultural, economic, and demographic forces that brought about this erosion fed the polarization of values and attitudes that has come to be so prominent a feature of the political scene.

It is true that, like all political theories (as William James said of social theories), this one leaks at every joint. Advocacy groups, the media, and officeholders from solidly "red" or "blue" constituencies have a large stake in an ideologically polarized politics. Yet there is abundant evidence—from polls, from elections—that a growing body of voters prefers a less polarized politics. The resulting disconnect between voters and the political class is one of the more conspicuous, and puzzling, aspects of the contemporary American political scene.

Campaigning toward the center and then governing from the ideological edge has been typical of recent presidents. That was the case with Bill Clinton before his sobering 1994 congressional election experience. It was the case with George Bush before his sobering 2006 congressional election experience. Will it be the case with Barack Obama after his widely anticipated sobering 2010 congressional election experience?

Gilbert and Sullivan's observation in *Iolanthe* that "every boy and every gal/That's born into this world alive/Is either a little Liberal/Or else a little Conservative" needs a second look. For some years now, self-described independents have been at least equal to and often more numerous than self-described Democrats or Republicans. The role of independents in the elections of 2006, 2008, and 2009 is widely held to have been decisive. There is good reason to expect that this will be the case as well in the fall of 2010.[10]

Also worth rethinking is the inclination to see large social groups as unalterably locked into ideological mindsets. It is true that some do stubbornly adhere to fixed patterns of electoral behavior: African-Americans and Jews most notably. But pundit-talk of how the rich, seniors, women, evangelicals, Catholics, Hispanics, Gen-Y'ers and other social constructs will behave politically is subject to continuing modification, fed by the counter-evidence of actual behavior.[11]

The will-o'-the-wisp of a permanent party majority continues to lure political pundits and gurus. But the electoral and cultural basis for that scenario is weak. The more accurate contemporary template is of an electorate with partisan and ideologically committed bell curve tails, and a substantial, growing, and politically determinant middle that is inclined to vote on the basis of the candidate and/or the issues more than the party.[12]

■ ■ ■

What about that distinctive new feature on the political scene, vocal and well-financed special interests? These include the traditional business-labor-farmer economic triad and also the growing number of social-cultural advocacy groups who constantly challenge the parties as political proposers and disposers.

Ideologically minded advocacy groups are widely regarded as the most conspicuous new force in American politics. Their political action committees and so-called 527 organizations reached a peak in money spent and attention garnered in the 2004 election. But the 2008 contest, and political developments since, highlight the volatility of contemporary American political culture. Left-wing fat cats such as George Soros and politically ambitious bloggers such as Markos Moulitsos and his Daily Kos, and Arianna Huffington and her Huffington Post, turned out to be flash-in-the-pan influences.

In this (as in much else) they resemble counterparts in the evangelical-fundamentalist Religious Right or conservative-populist talk show hosts Rush Limbaugh and Glenn Beck. All attract followings ample enough to pad their egos and their wallets, but hardly enough to control the political process. The inability of the GOP Right to block the nomination of Senator John McCain, and the predominance in 2008 of Obama's own fund-raising and support-getting operation over the advocacy groups, the blogosphere, the 527s, and organized labor, are evidence that the reach and staying power of fringes right and left have been exaggerated.[13]

The rise of Obama demonstrates the continuing capacity of our mainstream political system to reinvent itself. But it is subject to the iron law of diminishing returns. His 13 million or so online supporters have not as yet been successfully mobilized to be a force for his legislative program, as they were for his election.

Instead, the most notable (and least expected) turn of the political wheel has been the rise of the anti-big-government Tea Party movement, which has echoes of the Ross Perot episode of 1992. But the Tea Party has not yet demonstrated the staying power to be a significant force in the 2010 and 2012 elections.[14]

The bottom line appears to be that interest/advocacy group politics and populist political outbursts such as the rise of the Obama coalition in 2008 and the Tea Party in 2009–2010 are likely to be as transient and ephemeral as those widely touted previous game-changers the PACs, the 527s, the right-wing talk show hosts, and the left-wing blogosphere.

One way of making sense of this new political culture is to see it as shaped by an ongoing struggle between its major components. One of these is a two-party system ordained and legitimized by the Constitution—in effect, the only way we have of doing our political business. The other is the more variable political style generated by changing technology and a vast, mobile population ever subject to new demographic and social-economic conditions.

■ ■ ■

Finally, what about the media, whose political presence includes not only the press and television but those explosive new players the Internet and the blogosphere?

The Democratic-liberal inclination of the mainstream print and TV media is one of the more notable features of late twentieth and early twenty-first century political discourse. While media ownership shifted from opinionated (and usually right-wing) press barons to grayer corporate suits, reporters got to be more highly educated, more attracted to engaged and adversarial than to just-the-facts reporting, more likely to be Left-liberal in their social and political outlook. This did not occur in a cultural vacuum. It was linked to, and bolstered by, a similar shift in the makeup and outlook of colleges and universities, foundations, and other culture-definers.[15]

In life as in physics, every action has a reaction. The Left-liberal tone of the mainstream media and like-minded Web sites and blogs was not likely to flourish unchallenged in a predominantly centrist-conservative nation. Technology is wedded to no particular agenda, and in this case it made the liberal-mainstream media supremacy a brief one.

Talk radio was a cheap and widely accessible outlet for the rise of a conservative-right wing counter-voice. So too were the Internet and the blogosphere. Liberal-leaning CNN capitalized on the rise of cable TV. But it was soon confronted, and eventually outgunned, by conservative-leaning Fox News.

Meanwhile, the mainstream media—big city newspapers, the national news magazines, the three national television networks—eroded financially under the competitive pressure of cable TV and the Internet. From 2001 to 2008, newspapers declined as the major source of news of from 50 percent to 35 percent of the population. Television slid from 82 percent to 70 percent, while the Internet rose from 13 percent to 40 percent. The shrinking newspaper and TV news-viewing habits of Americans in the eighteen to twenty-nine-year-old age group suggests that this will be a continuing fact of American public life.[16]

But just as the major parties are able to retain their oligopolistic predominance over American politics (indeed, third parties are at a historic low), so the demise of the traditional media has been prematurely assumed. Television and the movies retain much of their popularity in the face of newer technologies. And it is not at all clear that supposed culture-changers such as the social networking sites Facebook and MySpace are about to transform the form and substance of American politics. An awful lot of old wine—what leads people to their political allegiances, the persistent need and hunger for news about the world outside, the continuing capacity of the parties to respond to the political needs of most people—sloshes around in the shiny new wineskins of the Internet Age.[17]

It is in this new political world that Obama brilliantly made his way to the presidency. And it is in this world that he must deal with the ideological, policy, and political realities that make governing so heavy a weight to bear.

IDEOLOGY

More so than for any president since Ronald Reagan, the question of Obama's ideology has been a conspicuous concern of the punditry. The Right (echoing its reaction to FDR seventy years earlier) fears that he nurtures a socialist agenda. The Left fears that he does not.

Obama's initial rhetoric and behavior confirmed the concerns of the Left more than the Right. He soothingly said in his Inaugural Address that the issue was not whether government was too big or too small, but whether or not it worked. True, this was more ambiguous than Clinton's declaration that the era of big government was over or Carter's warning: "Government cannot solve our problems. It cannot eliminate poverty, or provide a bountiful country, or reduce inflation, or save our cities, or cure illiteracy, or provide energy." But Obama's predecessors said these things well along in their administrations, when the political cost was clear of trying to push a social democratic state on a centrist country in non-parlous times.

It may be, as columnist Peggy Noonan suggested at the end of 2009, that Obama is in the process of moving from the Left to the center. For all the discontent fed by the recession, the state of the nation perhaps is not so different from what John F. Kennedy faced when in 1962 he told a Yale audience: "What is at stake in our economic decisions today is not some grand warfare of rival ideologies which will sweep the country with passion, but the practical management of a modern economy." Yet as his administration progresses, Obama stubbornly resists the temptation to succumb to the lure of ordinary policies for ordinary times.[18]

The Great Depression, opening the gates of political opportunity to labor and the new immigrants and their children, and the vast national bonding experience of the Second World War gave shape, meaning, and

permanence to the New Deal and the Rooseveltian political revolution. The Kennedy assassination and the
civil rights revolution did the same thing on a smaller
scale for Lyndon Johnson's Great Society. A similarly
substantial social context is not yet evident in the age of
Obama. As one of his supporters concedes, "The thirties
or the sixties it ain't." What he has to offer his core
supporters—African-Americans, the college young, affluent liberals—is more symbolic than substantive.

This unfavorable environment has not helped to clar-
ify what Obama is really about. Is he in the social democratic tradition of the New Deal, as modified by post-
1960 American liberalism and the European model? Or
is he essentially in the pragmatic, try-one-thing-and-
then-another spirit that also was part of FDR and the
New Deal, and indeed of the Democratic reform tradition? Is his a seat-of-the-pants statism that is in fact little
more than a gussied-up American pragmatism? After
all, to say of him, as RealClearPolitics's David Paul
Kuhn did, that "[w]e still don't know this President's
core," is hardly unknown in the annals of the modern
American presidency.[19]

▪ ▪ ▪

But it takes more than the president to define the place
of ideology in the American political scene. In the course
of the 2008 election campaign, there was much pars-
ing of the ideological division in the Democratic Party.
Hillary Clinton was seen as the spokeswoman of the
more moderate and temporizing wing in the tradition of

Bill Clinton and the Democratic Leadership Council. A younger, more Left-leaning "progressive" wing was supposedly led by Obama.

But is there so evident a split between tired, aging, late-twentieth-century Clintonian liberals on the one hand, and a fresh, progressive Obama mindset, altogether Now, on the other? Not so as anyone would notice. The new progressives have been much more into demonizing the Right (Bush, Cheney, Palin, the Tea Partiers) than developing an updated Left-liberal political outlook for the Age of Obama. Their natural stamping ground, the blogosphere, is by its very nature not conducive to informed and sustained analysis. Old Left standbys like *The Nation* and *The New Republic* suffer from circulation problems. (Their respiratory and neurological systems aren't in great shape either.) Hollywood's hard Left running dogs Michael Moore and Oliver Stone have marginalized themselves into the thankless roles of trying to put a fair face on such unsightly objects as Cuba's Castros and Venezuela's Hugo Chavez.

Yet progressives are increasingly displeased with what they see as Obama's drift from the faith. In this they echo the disillusionment of Republican conservative purists with the previous Bush administration's spending habits and taste for active government.

The most conspicuous current disappointment is that "a progressive era has not burst forth." This is blamed not so much on Obama's shortcomings as on the lack of a "vibrant Left movement" of the sort fostered by the labor movement and American radicalism in the 1930s, or by the civil rights and anti-Vietnam War crusades of the 1960s.[20]

The conditions necessary for the sea change the Left seeks are not readily visible. The 13 million or so Obama supporters in 2008 who were ardent enough to sign up, give money, and work for their candidate have not yet emerged as the advance guard of a new progressivism.

True, they both foster and feed on Obama's taste for chiliastic rhetoric, brilliantly combined with his cool persona. And he is more popular than his policies. But his emotive politics is difficult to harness to concrete ends. Obamaites are too diverse in their character and interests. In the cold light of governance, disillusion was inevitable.[21]

And there is a larger problem. The centrist-conservative bent of most Americans is a fact of long standing. A Gallup poll at the end of 1936, after FDR's landslide victory, found that since the election, 50 percent of respondents considered themselves more conservative, 15 percent more liberal, and 35 percent unchanged. FDR nevertheless turned left, to his considerable political cost in 1938.

A similar poll eight days after LBJ's comparable sweep in 1964 revealed that a healthy 58 percent favored the liberal position on issues. But when asked about their general political disposition, the resulting 37 percent liberal-34 percent conservative division was much closer. And the 1966, 1968, and 1972 election results soon showed how shaky was popular support for Great Society (or any other) liberalism.

From 2006 to 2010 the ideological split has been stable: 21–24 percent liberal, 35–37 percent moderate, 39–44 percent conservative. A Gallup poll in July 2009, while the Obama rose was still in bloom, came up with the cautionary finding that 39 percent of respondents said that their views had grown more conservative since Obama came into office. Only 18 percent said they had become more liberal.[22]

The Left's persistent belief that a popular breakthrough is imminent is touching in its resolute privileging of hope over experience. As humorist Will Rogers said of a dismally unsuccessful attempt in 1927 to mobilize "the better element" and rid Chicago of its corrupt GOP machine, "the trouble is, there ain't much of a better element in Chicago."

■ ■ ■

Republicans have shown a recurring incapacity to take advantage of this national disposition. True, there are a few GOP politicians and a covey of pundits (John McCain occasionally, as well as David Frum, David Brooks, and Ross Douthat) who have sought to set the party on a more centrist and moderate course.

It is widely held that Republicans, more unified and less numerous than the Democrats, are more likely to be subject to the dictates of ideological purity. That is arguable. The Left's assault on Joe Lieberman for supporting the war in Iraq was fully up to the high toe-the-line standards of the Right. But it cannot be said that what passes for political discourse on the Right is any improvement over what goes on in the Left. Neither popular culture nor the new media technologies are conducive to anything resembling the standards that the Founders, Lincoln, the Roosevelts, Kennedy, or Reagan set for the public forum.[23]

In a vivid demonstration of the law of unintended consequences, the most notable ideological response to the coming of the Age of Obama was not a new birth of American liberalism or progressivism—no Age of Jackson, Progressive Era, or New Deal—but a surging anti-government, conservative populism. Its signposts have been the town hall meetings of August 2009; the Tea Party movement and GOP victories in the Virginia and New Jersey governorships and the contest for Ted Kennedy's Massachusetts Senate seat of late 2009 and early 2010; and ambitious new conservative fund-raising groups such as American Crossroads and American Action Network, modeled on the left-wing America Coming Together (ACT), MoveOn, and Media Fund of 2006–2008. Despite fierce media disapproval, the amorphous Tea Party movement continued to show political muscle in the spring 2010 primaries. It is as though the coming of FDR was most notable not so much for the New Deal and the Roosevelt Coalition, but for the rise of the anti-New Deal American Liberty League.

The roots of this conservative populism lie not in its nineteenth and early twentieth century counterparts but in the reaction to the welfare state liberalism of the late twentieth century: the "red" state side of the culture war of the past half century. It surfaced in the Goldwater and George Wallace boomlets of the 1960s and in the inchoate but substantial Ross Perot upsurge of the 1990s. How large a splash the Tea Party can make in national politics is a question. Historical precedent weighs against it. But like its forerunners, it can leave its mark on the rhetoric and ideas of major party politics.[24]

Despite substantial evidence that moderation is the high road to political success, the pressures for ideological line-drawing on both the Left and the Right remain high. Just as George W. Bush's campaign rhetoric of compassionate conservatism was submerged by the political frenzy stirred by the 2000 election and the Iraq war, so has Obama's campaign mantra of post-partisanship been submerged by the content and politics of his legislative agenda.

The same visceral forces that drove the Republican Congresses of the Bush years to an ultimately self-destructive partisanship appear to be at work on Obama and his Democratic legislature. Middle-of-the-road *New York Times* columnist David Brooks detected in early March 2009 "a transformational liberalism that should put every centrist on notice." GOP pundit Michael Gerson observed: "Given a historic opportunity to occupy the political center, to blur ideological lines, to reset the partisan debate through unexpected innovation, Obama has taken the most tired, predictable agenda in American politics—the agenda of congressional liberalism—and made it his own." Yet the view of a conservative critic—"Obama ran as a moderate in order to move America sharply to the Left"—is, with the substitution of "Right" for "Left" and "Bush" for "Obama," the gravamen of the Democratic indictment of the former president.[25]

Pressures for adherence to a narrowly defined party line flourish on both sides of the partisan fence. The influence of ideologically driven media, supporters, and donors frequently trumps the moderating dictates of the larger political culture. Loose party discipline and polarized congressional districts foster ideological assertiveness in the face of abundant polling and electoral evidence that this can incur political costs.

Democratic Speaker Nancy Pelosi and former GOP Majority Leader Tom DeLay turned out to be siblings under the skin when it came to slash-and-burn partisan leadership. Analyst Dick Morris summed up the current state of affairs: "You are either an Obama, Pelosi or [Senate Majority leader Harry] Reid clone or you are a Republican. That's the new two-party system."[26]

The question is whether the fraught political atmosphere—the manifest public distaste for politics-as-usual and politics-as-war—can overcome the forces that make for polarization. What makes this a difficult question to answer is that both sides of the equation—the partisan pressures for polarization and the popular distaste for the resulting politics—are products of the same loose, autonomous public culture that prevails today. And it is hard to say which is more unstable: the Obama coalition of blacks, the college young, organized labor, and upscale liberals; or the GOP amalgam of the country-club bourgeoisie, disaffected Tea Partiers, and angry white men. The bottom line is a politics very much up for grabs.

As is so often the case, the state of American politics finds an echo in larger developments in the Western world. Think of American progressivism and British liberalism in the early twentieth century, Reaganism and Thatcherism in the 1980s, Clintonism and Blairism in the 1990s. The election of Obama coincident with the Great Recession of the late 2000s may seem deviant when compared to the general turn to the center-Right in France, Britain, Germany, Italy, and Eastern Europe. Yet skepticism toward statism appears to be rising in the United States as in Western Europe.[27]

The case can be made that the populism of the Right is only slightly less evanescent than the progressivism of the Left. The tension between popular unease with too-proactive government and popular fear of what undiluted capitalism might inflict, combined with the inbred inclination of the political class to couch issues in stark ideological terms, may still have unpredictable political consequences.[28]

Polarization and the red-blue regional-cultural division has been for several decades the dominant theme in modern American political analysis. But more recently another perspective—one that reflects the persistent discord between political elites and public opinion—has come to the fore. A new culture war may be emerging: between advocates of the freest possible enterprise and the most limited possible government on one side, and advocates of the social democratic model of an active, interventionist, regulatory state on the other. Will the red-blue/war-peace issues of recent decades be subsumed by what Arthur C. Brooks of the American Enterprise Institute calls "a competition between the public sector and the private sector over who defines the work and the institutions that make a nation thrive and grow"?[29]

Another portent of change: seemingly solid advocacy groups of recent years show signs of losing clout. On the Right, these include the National Conference of Catholic Bishops, the National Right to Life Committee, and anti-gay-rights spokespersons; on the Left, the National Organization for Women, the American Civil Liberties Union, and groups focused on global warming.[30]

It does seem that the traditional benchmarks of political and ideological identity—ethnicity, race, region, class—are being gradually but inexorably replaced by the more diffuse and transient distinctions of generations, culture, religion, and ideology. Social issues that until recently seemed determinative—race, abortion, gay rights—are subject to these transformational social forces. The Democrats are no more most accurately described as the party of the people than the Republicans as the party of the rich.

But just as the Democrats run the risk of succumbing to a Left/liberal ideology substantially out of sync with prevailing American public attitudes, so are the Republicans at risk of remaining in thrall to a party ideology steeped in conspiracy theories of socialism. Obama's overreach more than GOP alternatives is what stirs voters; they are more repelled by the one than attracted by the other. A party of anger rather than ideas is an alluring but questionable way of confronting a party of liberalism; heartland populism is not enough. But whether by 2012 the Republicans will be the party of Mitt Romney or Sarah Palin, or (most likely) of some still-developing third force, has not yet reached the stage of informed speculation.[31]

▪ ▪ ▪

While it is difficult to imagine more apposite politicians than Obama and George W. Bush, it is unlikely that history (though one never knows about historians) will see their respective administrations as models of antithetical modes of governing.

In domestic policy, health care reform sharply separates the records of the two. (Although even here the resonance of Bush's prescription drugs add-on to Medicare and the still-uncertain future of Obamacare dictates caution.) Their responses to the economic downturn sharply differed in emphasis, but conjoined in the initial reaction to the banking crisis. Obama wants to amend the No Child Left Behind Act, not repeal or reverse it. When it comes to spending on education, health care, and infrastructure, their differences are of scale more than substance, if the complaints of conservatives that Bush spent too much and of liberals that Obama is spending too little are to be given credence.[32]

Much the same can be said of foreign policy. Obama may make nicer, and he certainly makes nice more effectively, to the Europeans, Islam, and other dicey "partners" than Bush did. But it is by no means clear that his nicety has led to strong new policy paths—by us or by them—in realms stretching from Iraq-Afghanistan-Iran to Russia-China-North Korea.

The first year-plus of the Obama administration was dominated by the character and passage of signature legislation. This will be subject increasingly to the 2010 congressional and state elections and, beyond that, the presidential election of 2012. If the first stage of the Obama years was dominated by the heaviness of governing, the next one is bound to focus on the no less weighty (but more comfortably familiar) task of winning elections.

We may expect, too, that a number of policy chickens, foreign and domestic, let loose from the Obama henhouse will come home to roost, with consequences both substantive and political that are still elusive. It is to this developing realm of policy and politics that we turn.

CHAPTER

Unfinished Business: Policy and Politics

P REDICTING THE FUTURE COURSE of the Obama administration is at best a formidable task. To attempt to do so as a historian compounds the difficulty. Even political scientists, when the chips are down, know better than to venture too far out on the prognostication branch of their disciplinary tree. Two of the field's more popular aphorisms: (1) it's best to predict an event after it happens; (2) while none of us predicted it, all of us can tell you why it was inevitable.

Given this, what can be expected of Clio's crystal ball, cloudy at best but positively opaque when the object of contemplation is so close at hand, so resistant to History's fuzzed but comforting perspective? Historian Charles Beard once said that writing history was like dragging a tomcat by its tail across a Brussels carpet. How much truer that is when the weavers are still hard at work on a product whose ultimate character neither they nor anyone else can readily forecast.

POLICY

Among the most important but least predictable factors in estimating the probable path of the Obama administration is the changing character of the issues that define the substance and shape the course of public policy.

On the domestic side of the agenda, it seems highly probable that the primary public concerns will continue to be economic and fiscal: more precisely, unemployment, and government spending and indebtedness. Energy and greenery, what (if anything) to do about illegal immigration, and education reform are likely to find it difficult to attain more than intermittent and parochial attention in the pecking order of national issues. It is suggestive that in the spring of 2010 there was talk of a shift of administration priorities from energy to immigration; but that was soon submerged by the sudden squall of the Gulf oil spill and ongoing angst over jobs and debt.[1]

It is not that large and vocal segments of the population do not care about these other matters or that the administration is reluctant to take them on. Indeed, the perceived political potential of concerns such as the excesses of investment bankers, the well-entrenched middle class desire for clean and reliable energy, and the anti-Hispanic implications of the reaction to illegal immigration have been—and are likely to continue to be—prominent parts of the Obama agenda.

Nevertheless, as the 2010 election and the administration's halfway point draw near there are few signs that the dual concerns of joblessness and spending/debt are likely to be displaced at the epicenter of the national political consciousness. Indeed, as 2010 unfolds evidence mounts that the intertwined themes of overspending and too much debt are gaining traction.

One potentially explosive political expression of that concern is the juxtaposition of massive state and local deficits with a growing disparity between public and private employee salaries, pensions, and health care. For decades, states such as California, New York, Illinois, and New Jersey and cities such as New York and Los Angeles have been held hostage by an iron triangle of powerful public employee unions, complaisant state legislatures and city councils, and compliant governors and mayors. Out of this has come an ever-larger web of solid wages and even better health care and pension benefits.

When times were good, voters raised no strong objections. But in 2009, state budget shortfalls totaled $110 billion (a third of this in California alone), with the next fiscal year promising to be worse. At the same time, joblessness and employment insecurity, pay cuts, and shrinking benefits became ever more the norm in the private sector, while precisely the opposite was happening with public employment. One estimate at the end of 2009 was that government workers earned 21 percent more than their private counterparts, were

24 percent more likely to have health care coverage, and were far more likely (84 percent to 21 percent) to have guaranteed defined-benefit instead of chancy defined-contribution pension plans. An issue was born.[2]

This is likely to have the reverse of the political impact of the labor concerns of the 1930s. Beleaguered industrial workers, struggling for basic organizing and bargaining rights against intransigent employers, won wide public support and added substantially to the electoral clout of the New Deal. Now popular opinion is increasingly hostile to cosseted public employees and their unions, who are seen as further feathering well-furnished nests while private workers struggle. The money and campaign work of public sector union members, so important to recent Democratic political fortunes, run the risk of alienating a much larger non-public workforce.[3]

Signs of a taxpayers' revolt have begun to appear. A 2009 California referendum rejected every proposal calling for increased spending, but endorsed restraints on public service unions. Republican Chris Christie's gubernatorial victory in New Jersey drew heavily on the theme of out-of-control spending and over-compensated state employees. New York Democratic gubernatorial aspirant Andrew Cuomo thought it politic to make an investigation of public sector perks a keynote of his campaign.[4]

Another issue with large potential is foreign policy, that old savior (or graveyard) of beleaguered presidents. Obama entered office when foreign affairs for the first time in years had a secondary place in public life. His agenda focused primarily on major domestic issues: the financial crisis, the economy, health care, energy, the environment.

Iraq, once the centerpiece of Obama's criticism of the Bush administration, began to fade from view as the surge appeared to be working, and became a secondary issue as the state of the economy displaced all else. Foreign policy took on a retro tone in the campaign, dominated by reflexive Bush-bashing. Otherwise, Obama melded foreign affairs into his more general message of hope and revival, pledging himself to heal the country's Bush-bruised relations with the rest of the world.

Linking the Bush administration to both the Iraq war and the economic meltdown was a natural campaign theme. To conjoin these issues in a common style of governance was more difficult. From the first, it was an easier sell to blame Bush and the bankers for the economic crisis than to blame Bush for the war on terror.

As Iraq quieted, Obama was able to live up to his commitment to a drawdown. At the same time, the worsening security situation in Afghanistan reinforced his campaign mantra that it was al Qaeda in that country that should have been, and would be, the nation's prime concern.

He responded to requests for a substantial upgrading of America's military presence in Afghanistan with months of deliberation. His supporters favorably contrasted this with the from-the-hip decision-making of Bush. His detractors unfavorably contrasted it to Bush's forceful response to terrorism. But as his first year ended, Obama's Afghanistan policy appeared to be the most popular one on his agenda.[5]

There were less noticeable echoes of Bush-style foreign policy, of a piece with Obama's decision to commit some 30,000 additional troops to a (time-limited) Afghanistan intervention. One of these was his below-the-radar transfer of suspected terrorists to countries where a Marquess-of-Queensbury-like process of interrogation was not likely. Another was the increasingly robust use of pilotless drones and smart missiles, hallmarks of a new, sanitized war against terror.

This hardly met the expectations of Obama's antiwar base, however well it accorded with the demands of governing as distinct from electioneering. Other Obama actions were designed to right the balance. One was his reiterated promise (though with an increasingly loose timetable) to close the terrorist holding center at Guantanamo Bay. Another was a brisk round of speeches and summit meetings designed to assuage the grievances (real and imaginary) of the Muslim, Latin American, and Russo-Chinese worlds.

As Obama's Year One slid into Year Two, it became increasingly evident that counterparts to the constraints and contradictions afflicting his domestic agenda operated on his foreign policy as well. Here as there, expectations were dashed, results less than hoped for.

Obama sought to play a leading role in coordinating the response of the world's more consequential economies to the economic downturn. But this ran afoul of the intransigent facts of national self-interest and the recession-weakened bargaining position and growing isolationist sentiment in the United States.[6]

His manifestly sincere (to some, embarrassingly excessive) apologies for his nation's past misdeeds did seem to improve the general overseas perception of the United States. But it also appeared to feed the inclination of world leaders to think that with Obama, the American Hegemon had lost some of its capacity to shock and awe. There was talk of Obama echoing the "Carter Syndrome" of dithering in the face of provocation, speculation as to whether or not he was "tough enough."[7]

A disconnect emerged as well in the realm of climate change. As in the case of their damaged banking systems and heavy fiscal deficits, the industrial nations had a common stake in minimizing the adverse effect of global warming. But they also had a shared reluctance to adopt the constraints deemed necessary to reduce it. Once again, a common problem did not readily trump self-interested national responses.

How confined was Obama's capacity to lead on climate change (or, indeed, any other area) became evident at the best-forgotten Copenhagen conference in December 2009. Snubs from China (an echo of his dicey reception when he visited there) and a lack of substantive results reinforced the growing sense of his inability to forcefully impose himself in the foreign arena.

The Obama policy to change the tenor of the war on terror by greater outreach to America's enemies fared no better. A pattern of initial downplay and denial, followed by acceptance that this was, indeed, Terrorism at Work, characterized the administration's reactions to the killings at Fort Hood and the would-be Detroit plane bomber. And then there was the political backlash to the decision to try 9/11 overseer Khalid Sheikh Mohammed in a New York City civilian court, a misstep that as of this writing has not been formally reversed.

The questions asked of Obama's larger foreign policy goals have a close family relationship to those raised about his domestic agenda. In both realms there is a persistent fear among conservatives and increasing numbers of moderates, and hope against hope among liberals, that he is set on large-scale policy change. At home the model is a substantially more active federal government, echoing the European social-democratic example. Abroad it is a post-Cold War, post-War on Terror policy with a stronger outreach to China, Russia, and the Muslim world, and less confrontation with states such as Iran, Syria, and Venezuela.

Obama could make a credible case that in fact he has hewed to the main lines of modern American foreign policy. His withdrawal plan from Iraq differs little from that of his predecessor Bush. And it is difficult to see that Bush would have followed a significantly different path in Afghanistan.

It is true that Obama for a while changed the tone of American rhetoric toward rogue states and drew back from the traditional close ties with Israel. But it is also true that the incidents that lend credence to the view that his is a new foreign policy have been followed by words and acts reiterating the established American foreign policy canon.

It is not clear to what degree the bimodal character of much of Obama's diplomacy is due to his own predilections and to what degree it reflects divisions within his administration's ranks and the noticeable anti-Israel, anti-war-on-terror sentiment of many of his supporters. Bush had to deal with comparable, though ideologically opposite, gung-ho sentiments among what the media labeled neoconservatives.

Obama's privileged position in the mainstream media has shielded him so far from the hyperbolic criticism leveled at Bush's foreign policy. But it is also the case that there has not been an attention-focusing event on his watch comparable to 9/11 or the Iraq war. Obama's foreign policy is a work in progress. It has not racked up the successes it seeks: a Middle East settlement, an end to the Iranian nuclear weapons program, America restored to the Third World's good graces (assuming it ever resided there). Nor has it encountered the disasters its critics expected. But given Obama's predilection for large goals and elevated rhetoric, a major foreign policy challenge may very well evoke an expansive, Wilsonian response.[8]

POLITICS

What is likely to determine Obama's first big political test, the November 2, 2010 election? This is not a time when the range of the politically possible is unusually wide, such as the Great Depression of the 1930s that set the stage for the New Deal, or the JFK assassination, the civil rights movement, and the 1964 election that set the stage for the Great Society. Popular support for large change does not match the ambition of Obama and his more fervid supporters. A poll in January 2010 revealed public disapproval of some of his major policy positions: by 53 percent to 40 percent on health care, 48 percent to 41 percent on terrorism, 49 percent to 28 percent on immigration. But majorities supported him on Afghanistan, Iraq, Social Security, education, and the environment. There is little evidence that attitudes have changed much since then.[9]

Perhaps the biggest unanswered policy questions are the degree of big government that Americans want or will accept, and the extent to which a strongly ideological president can or will adapt to uncomfortable political realities. In neither case is a resolution predetermined. These are, after all, matters of policy nuance, not black-or-white choice. Nor is it difficult for even the most skilled politicians to misread their situation: FDR in the recession of 1937–1938 and LBJ in the Vietnam-urban riot years of 1966–1968 come to mind.

It should be recognized (though the media and the commentariat for the most part are not inclined to do so) that Obama, like his predecessors, is part of an established political culture of strong, self-contained interest and advocacy groups, often with solid representation in Congress. This is hardly novel. FDR (and less so LBJ) had to balance off Southern and Northern Democratic congressional wings which were more often at each others' throats than in each others' pockets. Obama too has to cope with a Congress which, while strongly Democratic, is divided along regional, cultural, and ideological lines.[10]

Nor should it be forgotten that the cultural and institutional sources of the heavy weight of governing are hardly unique to Obama. George W. Bush campaigned in 2000 as a consensus-builder, based on his record as governor of Texas. The bitter election tarnished that image. The coming together that followed 9/11 was an opportunity to refurbish it. But the Iraq invasion and hubris engendered by the 2002 and 2004 elections fed ideological line-drawing that had harmful political consequences for the GOP.[11]

Conspicuous polarization in the face of widespread popular distaste for ultra-partisanship has been a fact of American political life at least since the 1960s. Obama like Bush has not yet engaged in any real effort to build bridges across the party divide, except on his own terms. Bush in fact got more Democratic support for some of his major efforts (No Child Left Behind, the Patriot Act, Medicare prescription coverage) than Obama could for his signature economic stimulus, health care, and financial reform bills. The disconnect between public expectations and the ideological objectives of the administration, an erosive force in the Bush years, seems to be playing out once again as Obama approaches his mid-term test.

At the beginning of the Obama presidency two presidential scholars cautioned him to avoid alienating citizens from their government, as Bush had done. It can be argued that this is precisely what has happened. But that this is so may more usefully be ascribed to the character of modern American political culture than to the character of Obama.[12]

Like Clinton and Bush II before him, Obama has had to face and deal with the core tension between an assertive ideological base and a considerably more centrist American electorate. His 2008 victory was solid but not sweeping. While the popular desire for "change" was palpable, there was little reason to think that this was a mandate to govern from the Left, any more than Bush's electoral victories were a mandate to govern from the Right.

The at-best tepid public reaction to Obama's signature accomplishments—the stimulus, health care, and financial reform—testify to that. So does abundant polling evidence that liberal-leaning voters are substantially outnumbered by conservative-leaning ones, and that those defined as independents, widely seen as determining the 2006 and 2008 elections, have moved substantially away from their pro-Obama leanings.

But this by no means assures the triumph of the recent Tea Party-driven conservative populism. The game-deciding independents shy from angry conservative populists as they do from angry Left-liberals.[13]

The Voice of History is clear on the likelihood of an off-year electoral falloff for the Democrats. But it is decidedly muted as to the scale of the political harm he will suffer. Have the post-2008, pre-fall 2010 elections given any signals? So far the consensus has been: Yes. The Virginia and New Jersey Republican governorship wins in late 2009 and Scott Brown's super-hyped taking of Ted Kennedy's Massachusetts Senate seat in early 2010 set the tone.

The electoral equivalent of pigeon entrails multiplied in the spring of 2010. Signs and portents included the rejection of three-term Senator Robert Bennett by Utah Republicans; the victory of Tea-Party-backed Rand Paul (son of Texas Libertarian Ron) over the GOP establishment candidate in the Kentucky senatorial primary; and Representative Joe Sestak's defeat of Republican-turned-Democrat Arlen Specter in Pennsylvania's Democratic senatorial primary.

But while the theme of voter discontent commands general assent, just how this will play out in the fall of 2010 remains the subject of partisan spin more than broader analysis. The Tea Party is calling the turn in the GOP! The unions and MoveOn.org (who backed Sestak and helped keep Senator Blanche Lincoln from a first-round Arkansas primary victory) are calling the turn in the Democratic Party! Massive voter distaste for elected officials foretells a sweeping repudiation of (mostly Democratic) incumbents! Union money and clout, the moneyed Left blogosphere, and GOP intimacy with Tea Party fanaticism will contain or avoid an anti-Democratic sweep![14]

The common view is that the Republicans this fall will largely benefit from the normal attrition of the party in power and from a broad popular reaction against massive spending and the expansion of government.

It does seem beyond argument that as the polarized political culture of the past half-century took form, so did a recurring, usually inchoate public reaction to politics-as-usual, all too often defined as overstaying in office, sexual and monetary misbehavior, and a propensity to lie. Obama was right—perhaps more right than he knew—when he attributed Scott Brown's Massachusetts victory to the same discontent "that swept me into office."[15]

Like his predecessor George Bush, Obama has found it difficult to build a reliable political majority in a political environment where the traditional bonds of party discipline are substantially weakened. He has called on what he regards as his core coalition of 2008—blacks and Latinos, women, affluent liberals, the college young—to come together again in 2010. But this is to build on shifting sands. Lyndon Johnson observed that he was driven out of office by the young, blacks, and academics: precisely the core of the Obama coalition. The eighteen-to-twenty-five-year-old age group was the strongest cohort in Ronald Reagan's 1984 victory—and John Kerry's strongest cohort in his 2004 defeat. It is no longer the case that the Democrats can depend on solid, reliable support from white Southerners, immigrants, working class men, and Catholics. Nor can the Republicans rely on the business and professional classes and Protestant white collar workers.

If the Republicans are beset by their difficulty in appealing to numerically toothsome groups such as Hispanics and the young, the Democrats are bedeviled by the difficulty of selling their liberal-Left party program to a nation that leans moderate-conservative. These are not like the more stable factors of section, ethnicity, and class that defined the older party system. In their lack of clear definition ("Catholics" may be a fuzzy category—but compared to "the young"?) and the built-in instability of an explosively changing culture, the building blocks of contemporary politics are of doubtful solidity.

Many Democrats in Congress represent districts that normally vote for Republican candidates. What happens there is likely to depend not on a return to Republican roots but on how the decisive independent vote goes and how largely it participates. In this post-party age, that is an imponderable both large and difficult to control.[16]

Elections, like presidencies, are tempting subjects for historical analogy. The congressional election of 2010 evokes a number of possible comparisons. (See table, Congressional Elections, 1914–2006, on page 153.)

This adds up to thirteen elections, seven in the premodern era (1914–1958), six in the time of the current political culture (1966–2006). That is a lot of history to absorb. But we can narrow the field. There are first-term by-elections—1914, 1930, 1946, 1966, 1978, 1982, 1994—when economic downturns and/or perceived presidential insufficiency feed rejection. And there are mature-administration setbacks—1918, 1938, 1950, 1958, 1974, 2006—when voter weariness and/or presidential blunders shape the result.

Which of these are most resonant for 2010? Choose your politics and take your pick. Those awaiting with anticipation a one-term Obama presidency might like the look of the precursors of a national turnover: 1918, 1958, 1966, 1974, 1978, 2006. Those who dread that prospect might prefer something along the relatively mild midterm setbacks of 1978 or 1982, or the recovery of the incumbent parties after their 1914, 1938, 1946, 1984, and 1994 defeats.

A more analytical historical perspective should take into account the general standing of the president, his program, and his party; the makeup of the sources of public discontent; and the appeal (or lack of appeal) of the opposition. From that point of view, it might seem that, as of now, 1978 and 1982 are most relevant to the current state of affairs. The first was followed by incumbent Jimmy Carter's defeat, the second by incumbent Ronald Reagan's recovery: leaving us, quite properly, ambivalent as to Obama's future prospects.

His favorability ratings are about the same as Carter's were in 1978. Comparable too is the limited popularity of their programs and the general public dissatisfaction with politics-as-usual. On the other hand, Reagan in 1982, like Obama today, was strongly supported by his supporters and disfavored by his detractors. Economic issues—in particular, unemployment and the deficit—figured largely in public opinion. Reagan then,

Year	House	Senate	Comment
1914	R + 59	D + 5	Recoil from the GDP split of 1912; Democratic benefit from the direct election of Senators
1918	R + 19	R + 6	A reaction to Wilson's wartime state
1930	D + 52	D + 8	The Depression and Hoover's unpopularity
1938	R + 71	R + 6	Recession and FDR's executive excesses (e.g., Supreme Court packing plan)
1946	R + 55	R + 13	1918-like reaction against wartime controls and postwar inflation
1950	R + 28	R + 5	The Korean War, recession, and Truman-weariness
1958	D + 47	D + 13	Accumulated dissatisfaction with two terms of GOP governance
1966	R + 47	R + 3	Growing opposition to Vietnam War and Great Society legislation. LBJ: "A lot of our people don't belong here, they're in Republican seats, and the Republicans will get them back."[17]
1974	D + 43	D + 3	Watergate, etc., produce a near-mirror image of 1966
1978	R + 15	R + 3	Inflation, energy, and doubts about Carter, countered by doubts about the post-Nixon GOP
1982	D + 27	−	Unemployment and deficits earn Reagan a similarly mild rebuke
1994	R + 54	R + 8	Clinton's liberal domestic arm-flexing is massively repudiated
2006	D + 31	D + 6	Bush's Iraq obduracy, conservative arm-flexing, and Katrina fiasco are heavily repudiated

as Obama quite possibly might do now, used his formidable communication skills to craft a message that lessened the extent of his party's losses.

Obama remains more popular than Bush was in 2006 (or, for that matter, Reagan was in 1982). But if he and his advisers choose to assume that they have on tap a natural, built-in majority that can override bad news and growing public disfavor, they run the risk of emulating the Bush-Cheney miscalculation of 2006.[18]

The big imponderable is the degree to which the Obama administration repairs or worsens its current public standing. This is beyond anyone's predictive powers. But 1978 and 1982 had another shared feature: the lowest House and Senate turnovers in our mini-history. The congressional swings over the course of the first seven elections in our list (1914 to 1958) averaged 47.2 in the House and 8.0 in the Senate. Over the course of the next six elections (1966 to 2006), the averages were substantially less: 36.1 and 3.8.

So while a Democratic Armageddon in 2010 is possible (think 1994), the local power that derives from congressmen's autonomy, and the considerable potential of the Republican Right to be as off-putting as the Democratic Left, lessens the likelihood of a sweep of 1930, 1936, 1946, or 1994 magnitude. This of course precludes continuing disasters on the domestic or foreign fronts.

■ ■ ■

Looking still further ahead to the presidential election of 2012, we can summon up a comparable historical shopping list of second-term triumphs and disasters. Johnson in 1964 and Nixon in 1972 benefited largely from the deviant political messages of Barry Goldwater and George McGovern. Clinton in 1996 and Obama in 2008 had the advantage of long-in-the-tooth opponents. The decline of unemployment, a sense that the economy was on the upswing, and the popularity of the incumbent made for FDR's 1936 and Reagan's 1984 triumphs.

As different as Obama is from Bill Clinton in character, style, and political persona, the fact remains that Clinton was elected in 1992 with 258 Democratic members of Congress and 57 senators, precisely the same as Obama's initial base of support. And he began his presidency as a young liberal-Left reformer championing health care reform as his first order of public business. Presumably this adds to the cogency and attractiveness of the Clinton mid-course correction as one for Obama to emulate. But it slights the no-less-controlling truth that Obama, like Wilson, Carter, and Reagan before him, is driven by an ambition that makes Clintonian triangulation a hard pill to swallow. A reluctance to change course is a recurring phenomenon among young presidencies, and Obama's so far fits that pattern.

Democratic pollsters Douglas Schoen and Patrick Caddell advise their party to move closer to the views of the Tea Party movement: a clear non-starter. Liberals like *The New Republic*'s John Judis and the *New York Times* argue that Obama's 2012 prospects depend on his pouring money into government projects—a second stimulus. This depends on the accuracy of the assumption that it is government spending that brings about economic healing. That may or may not be so; the economic history jury is still out on that one.[19]

It is true that FDR after 1938, Truman after 1946, Reagan after 1982, and Clinton after 1994 overrode political setbacks. But this was due as much to the course of domestic and international events (World War II, the cold war, economic improvement) as to their superior political insight. LBJ, Nixon, Carter, and Bush I had varying talents. But they had the shared misfortune not to have been as fortunate in the events of their times (Vietnam, Watergate, the energy and hostage crises, a strong third party candidate) as the others.

Chronic instability is as much a part of the contemporary political scene as is the uneasy cohabitation of ideologically polarized parties with a centrist-leaning electorate. It takes no great stretch of the imagination to perceive that polarization and public disenchantment—the two dominant facts of current American political life—however much at odds with each other, are interrelated and co-dependent.

What is the implication of this state of affairs for predictions of the electoral future? Nothing very promising. History and political science can only go so far in portraying the conditions of the current political scene. Any attempt at more precise prognostication is not likely to transcend the realms of divining and soothsaying. Contingency—the course of events, the reaction of leaders—is ever more determining in our political world.

OBAMA IN HISTORY

What, refracted through History's miniaturizing lens, can be said of the current state and likely future prospects of the Obama administration? Perhaps the most unexpected turn of events so far is the degree to which this paradigm-altering president has been confined within the iron cage of the prevailing political culture, and by the no less commanding dictates of domestic and international reality. That experience is reflected in the shift in media analogizing from FDR's Hundred Days to the Carter-or-Clinton choice of how to deal with plans gone awry. If the descent from rhetoric and vision to the reality of everyday political and governmental life has been painful to many of his followers, and perhaps to Obama himself, that has to do in part with the unrealistically high expectations that his followers (and Obama himself) initially entertained.

To a notable degree, Obama's ongoing encounter with the facts of public life has been marked by policies and practices that are . . . Bushian. Far more than most expected, the president speaks as Barack Obama and governs like George Bush.

Increased domestic oil production may be an evil, but (even in the face of the Gulf of Mexico oil spill) a necessary one. An inadequate government response to the Gulf disaster, like Katrina under Bush, is immediately encased in bureaucratic rear-protection. It turns out that there is, after all, a war to be won: if not (in so many words) with militant Islam, then at least with al Qaeda and, if pressed, with "terror." This appears to require military trials, aggressive wiretapping, secure places of imprisonment, rendition, remote-controlled drones and their inevitable collateral damage, and other Bushian tactics.

A gap between promise and performance, between campaign accusations and the realities of governing, is hardly unique to Obama. Bush's conservative Republicans were as restless with his spending too much as Obama's liberals are with his spending too little. Even Ronald Reagan, of blessed conservative memory, left a substantial gap between his goal of reduced government and the ineluctable reality of the ever-growing (or at least not shrinking) American State.

Can Obama, forced by necessity, contain government as Bush, forced by necessity, expanded it? Can he in fact override the ongoing disparity between what he says about banks, Wall Street, and big business, and how in fact he deals with them?[20]

▪ ▪ ▪

To end where we began: are there historical analogues that may help us better understand the Obama presidency thus far? The initial parallels with FDR's New Deal and LBJ's Great Society have come to seem chimerical. As the Obama administration has unfolded, other presidents, their causes, and their modes of governance come more readily to mind.

Jimmy Carter, perhaps? Tempting; but, finally, No. For all their similarities of personality and career, there is a greater capacity and substance to Obama. Carter never secured anything on the scale of the Stimulus Act, Obamacare, or financial reform. And Obama has not as yet incurred the odium that came to attach to Carter.

Ronald Reagan? For all their shared communicative skills, a yawning gulf separates their politics, ideology, and age. And it is far from clear that Obama will leave a comparable imprint on his party or on the political tenor of his time. As of now, an Obamaite progressive/liberal revolution is a far less likely prospect than the Reagan conservative revolution turned out to be.

Bill Clinton? Aside from their being the most recent Democratic presidents, he and Obama have little in common, either in personality or ideology. The public approved of Clinton's policies more than they approved of Clinton. Precisely the reverse is true of Obama.

Perhaps the most intriguing analogy is with Woodrow Wilson. There is in Obama the same almost serene, self-confident righteousness, the same mix of academic-professorial eloquence and no-holds-barred political craft. It is true that Obama's social democratic, Left-liberal world view is leagues away from Wilson's bed-rock Southern white Presbyterianism. But where they come together, from their antipodean origins, is in the political mind-set that in Wilson's time, and in Obama's time, is called progressivism.

The two progressivisms, separated by a century, in some ways couldn't be more different. True, Wilson's version, like Obama's, supported government oversight of large corporations and the banking system, and rested on a belief in governance by an educated elite. But he did not share Obama's social democratic world view. Rather, he was steeped in bedrock nineteenth century Democratic Party principles: free trade, white supremacy. Obama is from Chicago, not Georgia; was influenced more by Saul Alinsky than by Thomas Jefferson; is not only not anti-black, but *is* black.[21]

It is perhaps revelatory (whether inspirational or worrisome, depends on how you regard Woodrow Wilson) to see some of the earlier president in the current one. And there is much to be gained from a historical context that shows how and why the New Foundation is not the New Deal or the Great Society, and certainly not Wilson's New Freedom. (Indeed, is not yet even the New Foundation.)

Saying this makes clear how limited are the uses of historical analogy. Once again, the weight under which Obama labors derives not so much from his own qualities as from the uncertain tenor of the age. Perhaps what an exploration of historical context such as this most helpfully does is to put some flesh on those timeworn truths that there is not only a lot of ruin, but a lot of persistence, in the institutions of a nation. And that it is perhaps just as well, in a democracy, that the weight of governing should not be too bearable.

NOTES

INTRODUCTION

1. John Kenney, "The Unbearable Lightness of Leading," *New York Times*, March 6, 2010, confines itself to Obama's lack of physical weight.

2. Jacob Weisberg, "Young Man in a Hurry," *Newsweek*, Dec. 7, 2009; Rocco Landesman in State News Service, Oct. 21, 2009. Also from *Newsweek:* "above the country, above the world, he's sort of God." Obama himself did little to stanch the flow of hyperbole when he identified his ascension with the imminent turning of the tides, a cure for cancer, a world without nuclear weapons, and math and science made "cool again" for students.

3. Peter Baker, "For Obama, a New Deal or at Least a New Phrase," *New York Times*, May 15, 2009.

CHAPTER ONE

1. Quoted in "Obama's Health-Care Gamble," *Newsweek,* Jan. 11, 2010.

2. "The man who fell to earth," *Economist,* Jan. 23, 2010.

3. *Newsweek* [cover], Nov. 2, 2009.

4. "Coming down to earth," *Economist,* March 28, 2009, and "The man who fell to earth," ibid., Jan. 23, 2010.

5. "Where Clinton Turned Right, Obama Plowed Ahead," *New York Times,* Jan. 28, 2010; David Brooks, "Liberal Suicide March," *New York Times,* July 21, 2009.

6. "Obama Needs to 'Reset' His Presidency," *Wall Street Journal,* July 17, 2009; "After July's Turmoil, Obama Needs 'A New Chapter' in August," *Washington Post,* Aug. 9, 2009; David Brooks, "The Obama Slide," *New York Times,* Sept. 1, 2009.

7. "So Much Gasbaggery, So Little Time," *New Republic,* Dec. 3, 2009; "We Have the Hope. Now Where's the Audacity?" *Washington Post,* Aug. 30, 2009; Charles Krauthammer, "Obama, The Mortal," *Real ClearPolitics.com,* Sept. 4, 2009. But see David Brooks, "The Great Gradualist," *New York Times,* Aug. 27, 2009.

8. Peggy Noonan, "From 'Yes, We Can' to 'No! Don't'!" *Wall Street Journal,* Aug. 14, 2009; "A president grossly overplaying his hand," *Kansas City Star,* Aug. 8, 2009; Douglas Schoen, "Crunch Time for Obama," *FOXnews.com,* Aug. 7, 2009.

9. Karl Rove, "The President Is No B+," *Wall Street Journal,* Dec. 17, 2009.

10. John Heilemann, "Obama Lost, Obama Found," *New York Magazine,* Nov. 29, 2009. See also Morris P. Fiorina and Samuel J. Abrams, *Disconnect: The Breakdown of Representation in American Politics* (Norman, OK: University of Oklahoma Press, 2009); Morton Keller, *America's Three Regimes: A New Political History* (New York: Oxford University Press, 2007), Part Four.

11. *The Onion,* Nov. 16, 2009; *onespot.WSJ.com,* Jan. 24, 2010.

12. George F. Will, "Mitch McConnell Smiled?" *Newsweek,* Sept. 12, 2009; on FDR, Jonathan Alter, *The Defining Moment: FDR's Hundred Days and the Triumph of Hope* (New York: Simon & Schuster, 2006), 254, 271.

13. "White House revamps communications strategy," *Washington Post,* Feb. 15, 2010; David Brooks, "What's Next, Mr. President?" *New York Times,* Feb. 11, 2010.

14. Sidney Milkis and Jesse Rhodes, "Barack Obama, the Democratic Party, and the Future of the 'New American Party System'," *The Forum* (online), vol. 7, (2009), no. 1.

15. The most influential and accessible works on this point are Keith Krehbiel, *Pivotal Politics: A Theory of U.S. Lawmaking* (Chicago: University of Chicago Press, 1998) and David W. Brady and Craig Volden, *Revolving Gridlock: Politics and Policy from Jimmy Carter to George W. Bush, 2nd ed.* (Boulder, CO: Westview Press, 2005).

16. Michael Barone, "When Liberal Leaders Confront a Centrist Nation," *RealClearPolitics.com*, Aug. 13, 2009.

17. "The Californication of Government," *Economist*, Feb. 28, 2009.

18. "Shenanigans and seriousness," *Economist*, Dec. 20, 2008.

19. Matt Bai, "Taking the Hill," *New York Times Magazine*, June 7, 2009; "Obama lags behind predecessors on executive orders," *Washington Times*, Feb. 19, 2010.

20. "Obama Gives Speeches, Interviews But Few Press Conferences," *ABCNews.com*, Jan. 14, 2010.

21. "The American Debate: Why Obama Can't Pull an LBJ," *Philadelphia Inquirer*, July 26, 2009.

22. "For Obama Cabinet, A Team of Moderates," *Washington Post*, Dec. 20, 2008.

23. "Not Right, or Left, but Forward," *Wall Street Journal*, Dec 5, 2008; "Hugging Republicans Until It Hurts," *New York Times*, June 7, 2009; "Coming Down to Earth," *Economist*, March 28, 2009.

24. Michael Janeway, *The Fall of the House of Roosevelt: Brokers of Ideas and Power from FDR to LBJ* (New York: Columbia University Press, 2004); Walter Isaacson and Evan Thomas, *The Wise Men: Six Friends and the World They Made* (New York: Simon & Schuster, 1997).

25. Kenneth E. Morris, *Jimmy Carter, American Moralist* (Athens, GA: University of Georgia Press, 1997): 172ff. For a highly favorable examination of the Obamaites at work, see Jonathan Alter, *The Promise: President Obama, Year One* (New York: Simon & Schuster, 2010).

26. "Staff Chief Wields Power Freely, But Influence Comes with Risk," *New York Times*, Aug. 16, 2009; Alter, *The Promise*, 159–172.

27. "Obama's BFF," *New York Times*, July 26, 2009; "Why Obama needs Rahm at the top," *Washington Post*, Feb. 21, 2010; Noam Scheiber, "The Chief," *New Republic*, March 3, 2010; "Core Chicago Team Sinking Obama Presidency," *Huffington Post.com*, Feb. 7, 2010.

28. Emmett Tyrrell, "Obama's Carousel of Incompetence," *RealClear Politics.com*, Aug. 28, 2009; John Harwood and Gerald F. Seib, *Pennsylvania Avenue: Profiles in Backroom Power* (New York: Random House, 2008).

29. "Radicals to rule us all," *Washington Times*, April 6, 2010; "Embattled Environmental Aide Resigns," *Washington Post*, Sept. 6, 2009.

30. "Obama's Team: The Face of Diversity," *National Journal,* June 20, 2009; Daniel Henninger, "Obama's America: Too Fat to Fail," *Wall Street Journal,* June 1, 2009.

31. "Obama's Endless Czar List Now Includes a Domestic Violence Aide," *U.S. News & World Report,* June 29, 2009; "White House Czar Inflation Stirs Concern," *Los Angeles Times,* March 5, 2009; Bruce Ackerman, "A Role for Congress to Reclaim," *Washington Post,* March 11, 2009 is an Obama supporter's criticism of czar-making.

32. John D. Donahue, *The Warping of Government Work* (Cambridge, MA: Harvard University Press, 2008); Paul C. Light, *A Government Ill Executed: The Decline of the Federal Service and How to Reverse It* (Cambridge, MA: Harvard University Press, 2008); "A Tough Search for Talent," *Economist,* Oct. 31, 2009, 70.

33. "Obama's Mixed Signals on Openness," *Boston Globe,* Dec. 7, 2009.

34. "Obama and 'Special Interests'," *Wall Street Journal,* Nov. 3, 2009.

35. Mark Hyman, "Obama's Enemies List Grows," *American Spectator,* June 8, 2009.

36. "The Battle Is Joined; Now What?" *New York Times,* Oct. 18, 2009; Patrick Caddell and Douglas E. Schoen, "Don't Shoot the Pollster," *Wall Street Journal,* Jan. 14, 2010.

37. "Eric Holder's Justice Department," *Weekly Standard,* Aug. 10, 2009.

38. Matt Grossmann, "Who Gets What Now? Interest Groups under Obama," *The Forum* [online], vol. 7 (2009) no.1; Keller, *America's Three Regimes,* 271–274.

CHAPTER TWO

1. Gary Dean Best, *Peddling Panaceas: Popular Economists in the New Deal Era* (New Brunswick, NJ: Transaction Publishers, 2005); Gary Becker and Kevin Murphy, "Do not let the 'cure' destroy capitalism," *Financial Times,* March 19, 2009.

2. Gary Becker et al., "Uncertainty and the Slow Recovery," *Wall Street Journal,* Jan. 4, 2010; "What went wrong with economics," *Economist,* July 18, 2009.

3. Gary Dean Best, *Pride, Prejudice, and Politics: Roosevelt versus Recovery, 1933–1938* (New York: Praeger Publishers, 1991): 89.

4. Allan Meltzer, "What Happened to the 'Depression'?" *Wall Street Journal*, Sept. 1, 2009.

5. Jonathan Alter, *The Defining Moment: FDR's Hundred Days and the Triumph of Hope* (New York: Simon and Schuster, 2006); Adam Cohen, *Nothing to Fear: FDR's Inner Circle and the Hundred Days that Created Modern America* (New York: Penguin Press, 2009).

6. "Summers: Banks must accept gov't regulation," *Seattle Times*, Oct. 16, 2009.

7. Jason Scott Smith, *Building New Deal Liberalism: The Political Economy of Public Works, 1933–1956* (Cambridge, MA: Cambridge University Press, 2005).

8. "How Big-Government is Obama?" *RealClearPolitics.com*, Jan. 9, 2009; "The Big Deal," *Washington Post*, Feb. 1, 2009; "The Big Fix," *New York Times*, Jan. 27, 2009; David Brooks, "Cleaner and Faster," *New York Times*, Jan. 29, 2009.

9. Morton Keller, *America's Three Regimes: A New Political History* (New York: Oxford University Press, 2007); Morris Fiorina, with Samuel J. Abrams, *Disconnect: The Breakdown of Representation in American Politics* (Norman, OK: University of Oklahoma Press, 2009); on Clinton, Keith Krehbiel, *Pivotal Politics: A Theory of U.S. Lawmaking* (Chicago: University of Chicago Press, 1998), 1–29.

10. "Judging a Stimulus by the Jobs," *New York Times*, Feb. 16, 2010; "White House to Mark Stimulus Anniversary with Progress Report," *Washington Post*, Feb. 18, 2010.

11. Obey quoted in "The Big Deal," *Washington Post*, Feb. 1, 2009.

12. On budget, "Fine Print: Funding Priorities and Targeted Savings," *Wall Street Journal*, May 8, 2009.

13. "Faith in Obama Drops as Deficit Fears Rise," *Washington Post*, Aug. 21, 2009; "Stimulus Remains Unpopular Even as It Boosts Growth," *Wall Street Journal*, Aug. 20, 2009.

14. "Money Stimulates Debate in States Over Plan's Goals," *Washington Post*, March 9, 2009.

15. "Holdren All Wrong," *Boston Herald*, Jan. 29, 2009.

16. "Benefits Requests Jump," *Wall Street Journal*, Nov. 9, 2009; "Job Question Jeopardizes Wind Farm's Stimulus Goal," *New York Times*, Nov. 6, 2009.

17. "Stimulus Watchdog Says White House Jobs Numbers May Not Be Accurate," *New York Times,* Nov. 20, 2009; "Obama Not as Honest as FDR," *Washington Times,* June 8, 2010.

18. "Out of work: The jobs bill is the latest close study in D.C. dysfunction," *Washington Post,* Feb. 14, 2010.

19. Irving Bernstein, *The New Deal Collective Bargaining Policy* (Berkeley: University of California Press, 1950); Milton Derber, ed., *Labor and the New Deal* (Madison: University of Wisconsin Press, 1957); Lizabeth Cohen, *Making a New Deal: Industrial Workers in Chicago, 1919–1939* (Cambridge, UK: Cambridge University Press, 1990).

20. Jonathan Alter, *The Promise,* 174–188, 91–92.

21. "Unions vs. Taxpayers," *Wall Street Journal,* May 14, 2009.

22. Michael E. Parrish, *Securities Regulation and the New Deal* (New Haven, CT: Yale University Press, 1970).

23. "Only a Hint of Roosevelt in Financial Overhaul," *New York Times,* June 18, 2009; "Credit cardholders' bill of rights," *Economist,* May 30, 2009.

24. Alter, *The Promise,* Ch. 18.

25. "Fannie, Freddie Losses May Hit US," *Wall Street Journal,* Jan. 22, 2010; "Ignoring the Elephant in the Bailout," *New York Times,* May 9, 2010.

26. "The Regulatory Rumble Begins," *Economist,* May 30, 2009; "Dodd's quest ends with financial overhaul," *Washington Post,* May 23, 2010.

27. "Dodd's Planned Retirement Muddles Financial Overhaul," *Wall Street Journal,* Jan. 7, 2010.

28. "A Decent Start," "Not All on the Same Page," *Economist,* July 3, 2010; "Law Remakes U.S. Financial Landscape," *Wall Street Journal,* July 16, 2010.

29. "Obama's Pledge to Tax Only the Rich Can't Pay for Everything, Analysts Say," *New York Times,* Aug. 1, 2009; "Health Care Reform and the Unpopular T-Word," *New York Times,* July 28, 2009.

30. "Redefining Capitalism After the Fall," *New York Times,* April 19, 2009; David Brooks, "Big-Spending Conservative," *New York Times,* April 21, 2009.

CHAPTER THREE

1. "ObamaCare and the Liberal Obsession," *Wall Street Journal*, Dec. 16, 2009; "Political Calculus," *RealClearPolitics.com*, Aug. 2, 2009; Edward D. Berkowitz, "The Scenic Road to Nowhere: Reflections on the History of National Health Insurance in the United States," *The Forum* [online], vol. 8 (2010), no. 1.

2. "Inside Interviews," *NationalJournal.com*, Feb. 18, 2010.

3. Roy Lubove, *The Struggle for Social Security, 1900–1935* (Cambridge, MA: Harvard University Press, 1968); Edward Berkowitz, *Mr. Social Security: The Life of Wilbur J. Cohen* (Lawence, KS: University Press of Kansas, 1995).

4. Edward Berkowitz, "Medicare: The Great Society's Enduring National Health Insurance Program," in Sidney M. Milkis and Jerome M. Mileur, eds., *The Great Society and the High Tide of Liberalism* (Amherst, MA: University of Massachusetts Press, 2005); John A. Andrew III, *Lyndon Johnson and the Great Society* (Lanham, MD: Ivan R. Dee, 1998), chap. 3.

5. "Medicare Is No Model for Health Reform," *Wall Street Journal*, Sept. 11, 2009.

6. Kenneth E. Morris, *Jimmy Carter: American Moralist* (Athens, GA: University of Georgia Press, 1996), 250ff.

7. Rachel L. Holloway, "The Clintons and the Health Care Crisis: Opportunity Lost, Promise Fulfilled," in Robert E. Denton, Jr., and Holloway, eds., *The Clinton Presidency: Images, Issues, and Communications Strategies* (Westport, CT: Praeger, 1996), chap. 8.

8. "New Ground for GOP with Kennedy's Unlikely Aid," *Washington Post*, Dec. 9, 2003; "Medicare Law's Costs and Benefits Are Elusive," *New York Times*, Dec. 9, 2003; "The Lessons of Medicare Part D," *Wall Street Journal*, Jan. 7, 2010.

9. Jonathan Alter, *The Promise: President Obama, Year One* (New York: Simon & Schuster, 2010), chap. 15.

10. Stephanie Condon, "Daschle, Dole Promote Bipartisan Health Care," *CBS News.com*, June 17, 2009.

11. "GOP Begins Nationwide Effort to Emphasize Policy Initiatives," *Washington Post*, May 1, 2009.

12. "CEOs Tally Health-Bill Score," *Wall Street Journal,* Oct. 19, 2009; "Winners and Losers in the Affected Industries," *Wall Street Journal,* March 27, 2010; "A Delicate Dance for 2 Health Lobbyists," *New York Times,* Oct. 27, 2009.

13. "Debate's Path Caught Obama by Surprise," *Washington Post,* Aug. 19, 2009; "Obama Offers Reassurance on Plan to Overhaul Health Care," *New York Times,* Aug. 12, 2009; "Back from the Dead," *Economist,* Oct. 31, 2009.

14. Janet Trautwein, "Why We Need a Strong Individual Mandate," *Wall Street Journal,* Nov. 11, 2009; "The Unhealthy Accounting of Uninsured Americans," *WSJ.com,* June 24, 2009; "One in Three Young Adults Is Uninsured," *KaiserHealthNews.org,* Feb. 25, 2010.

15. "Obama Initiatives Hit Speed Bumps on Capitol Hill," *Washington Post,* June 19, 2009; "Falling Far Short of Reform," *New York Times,* Nov. 10, 2009.

16. "House Haggles Over Abortion in Health Care Bill," *New York Times,* Nov. 4, 2009; "House Democrats pass health-care bill," *Washington Post,* Nov. 8, 2009.

17. "Last Call on Reforming Health Reform Bill," *New York Times,* Dec. 22, 2009; Bob Herbert, "A Less Than Honest Policy," *New York Times,* Dec. 28, 2009.

18. "Medicaid Expansion May Fail Because of Doctors' Refusal to See Patients," *BNET.com,* Nov. 29, 2009; "Prescription: more doctors," *Baltimore Sun,* Jan. 1, 2010; Jeffrey S. Flier, "Health 'Reform' Gets a Failing Grade," *Wall Street Journal,* Nov. 17, 2009; "Johns Hopkins Medicine and the Health Care Debate," *The Health Care Blog.com,* Nov. 5, 2009; John Mackey, "The Whole Foods Alternative to ObamaCare," *Wall Street Journal,* Aug. 11, 2009; "Medicare and the Mayo Clinic," *Boston Globe,* Jan. 6, 2010.

19. "States Resist Medicaid Growth: Governors Fear For Their Budgets," *Washington Post,* Oct. 5, 2009.

20. Fouad Ajami, "Obama's Summer of Discontent," *Wall Street Journal,* Aug. 25, 2009; "Conservatives Maintain Edge as Top Ideological Group," *Gallup.com,* Oct. 26, 2009.

21. Charles Krauthammer, "Obamacare in Retreat," *RealClearPolitics.com,* July 31, 2009.

22. Norman J. Ornstein, "Obama's Health-Care Realism," *Washington Post,* Sept. 1, 2009.

23. Bill Bradley, "Tax Reform's Lesson for Health Care Reform," *New York Times,* Aug. 29, 2009; Peter Ferrara, "The Republican Alternative," *American Spectator,* Nov. 18, 2009.

24. "Buoyant House Democrats Unveil Health Care Legislation," *New York Times,* Oct. 29, 2009.

25. Casey quoted in "Senate Democrats See Hope on Health Bill," *New York Times,* Dec. 9, 2009; Jonathan Chait, "And the Rest Is Just Noise," *The New Republic,* Dec. 24, 2009; Elizabeth Drew, "Is There Life in Health Care Reform?" *New York Review of Books,* March 11, 2010.

26. Alter, *The Promise,* chap. 22.

27. "Grit, deals, luck seal Obama's health care plan," *ABC News.com,* March 23, 2010.

28. David W. Brady and Daniel P. Kessler, "Why Is Health Reform So Difficult?" *Journal of Health Politics, Policy and Law* 35 (April, 2010), 161–176.

29. "Seizing the reins, at long last," *Economist,* Feb. 27, 2010; "Vote by Vote, A Troubled Bill Was Revived," *Wall Street Journal,* March 22, 2010.

30. "How Obama revived his health-care bill," *Washington Post,* March 23, 2010.

31. Fred Hiatt, "A Summer Obama Drama," *Washington Post,* Aug. 10, 2009.

32. "The Return of ObamaCare, Part I: The Legislative Context," *Real ClearPolitics.com,* Feb. 24, 2010; "The Return of ObamaCare, Part II: The Political Context," *RealClearPolitics.com,* Feb. 25, 2010.

33. Daniel Henninger, "Obama and the Old Hat People," *Wall Street Journal,* Oct. 29, 2009.

34. "In Health Care, Number of Claims Denied Remains a Mystery," *Huffington Post.com,* Sept. 18, 2009; "TV ad overstates health insurance denials," *politifact.com,* Sept. 18, 2009; "White House redirects health reform spotlight to insurance abuses," *amednews.com,* Aug. 24, 2009; "Most Popular Part of Obamacare is Redundant," *HealthCareNews.com,* June 2010; Robin Marty, "Wellpoint Responds to Criticism on Rescissions," *RHRealityCheck.com,* April 26, 2010.

35. Robert Samuelson, "Obama's proposal is the illusion of 'Reform',"
RealClearPolitics.com, March 15, 2010; Samuelson, "Planting the Seeds
Of Disaster," *RealClearPolitics.com*, March 29, 2010; "Pass the bill,"
Economist, March 20, 2010; "Now what?", "Signed, sealed, delivered,"
"From hope to change," "The health-care squeeze," *Economist*,
March 27, 2010.

36. William McGurn, "Saving the Obama Presidency," *Wall Street
Journal*, Aug. 24, 2009; David W. Brady et al., "Health Care Is Hurting
Democrats," *Wall Street Journal*, Jan. 19, 2010.

37. Mark Penn, "The Health Care Jam," *RealClearPolitics.com*,
March 8, 2010; Patrick H. Caddell and Douglas E. Schoen, "If Democrats
ignore health-care polls, midterms will be costly," *Washington Post*, March
12, 2010; "The Health Care Letdown," *New York Times*, March 15,
2010.

CHAPTER FOUR

1. David Broder, "End of the Honeymoon," *RealClearPolitics.com*,
March 15, 2009; "One Year of The One," *Economist*, Oct. 31, 2009; Ross
Douthat, "The Obama Way," *New York Times*, Dec. 25, 2009.

2. Frank Rich, "It's a Bird, It's a Plane, It's Obama!" *New York Times*,
April 3, 2010.

3. The most influential modern classification of presidential types is
Stephen Skowronek, *The Politics Presidents Make: Leadership from John
Adams to George Bush* (Cambridge, MA: Belknap Press, 1993). See also
Skowronek, *Presidential Leadership in Political Time* (Lawrence, KS: Uni-
versity Press of Kansas, 2008).

4. "The Sometimes-Tough President," *Wall Street Journal*, March 8,
2010; Robert Dallek, "Obama's Historic Health-Care Victory," *Wall
Street Journal*, Dec. 29, 2009.

5. Burton I. Kaufman and Scott Kaufman, *The Presidency of James
Earl Carter, Jr.* (Lawrence, KS: University Press of Kansas, 2006); Kenneth
E. Morris, *Jimmy Carter, American Moralist* (Athens, GA: University of
Georgia Press, 1996); Philip Jenkins, "The Spirit of '76: Welcome Back,
Carter," *American Conservative*, Dec. 15, 2008. More cautionary is Leslie
H. Gelb, "Obama's Jimmy Carter Problem," *Daily Beast*, Dec. 28, 2009.

6. Todd Estes, "Cautionary Tales from the Clinton Administration," *The Forum* (online), vol. 7 (2009), no. 1.

7. William Schambra, "Obama and the Policy Approach," *National Affairs*, no. 1 (Fall 2009).

8. Mark Mellman, "Some quick to write off Obama," *The Hill*, March 9, 2010; "Reality Bites," *The Economist*, Jan. 14, 2010; Niall Ferguson, "Just Imagine," *American Interest*, January-February, 2010, sees Obama as "a professor who likes to make policy in seminars."

9. David M. Kennedy, "FDR's Lessons for Obama," *Time*, June 24, 2009; Jay Cost, "Obama's Strategic Mistake," *RealClearPolitics.com*, July 8, 2009, argues that Obama had a clear election mandate to make the economy his first order of business.

10. Morton Keller, *America's Three Regimes: A New Political History* (New York: Oxford University Press, 2007), Part Four; Ronald Brownstein, *The Second Civil War: How Extreme Partisanship Has Paralyzed Washington and Polarized America* (New York: Penguin Press, 2007); Morris P. Fiorina, with Samuel J. Abrams, *Disconnect: The Breakdown of Representation in American Politics* (Norman, OK: University of Oklahoma Press, 2009).

11. "Two Parties Fleeing the Center," *Washington Post*, June 13, 2007; Fiorina, *Disconnect*.

12. "A Permanent Democratic Majority?" *RealClearPolitics.com*, April 15, 2009; "There Are No Permanent Majorities in America," *Real ClearPolitics.com*, July 2, 2009. See also John Podhoretz, "An Obama Realignment?" *Commentary*, December 2008, 132–137; Morton Keller, "An Election in History," *The American Interest*, January-February 2009, 88–93.

13. Keller, *Three Regimes*, chap. 12; Keller, "Election in History."

14. "Discontent's Demography: Who Backs the Tea Party," *New York Times*, April 14, 2010; William Voegeli, "The Meaning of the Tea Party," *Claremont Review of Books*, Spring 2010, 12–19.

15. Morton Keller, "The Media: What They Are Today, and How They Got That Way," *The Forum* (online), vol. 3 (2005), no. 1.

16. "Web Blows By Papers as News Source," *RealClearPolitics.com*, Dec. 26, 2008. On the decline of the print media, "Tossed by a gale," *Economist*, May 15, 2009.

17. "The rebirth of news," *Economist,* May 16, 2009; "The Shock of the Old," *Economist,* April 22, 2010, 55, on traditional media dominating the British election.

18. Peggy Noonan, "Obama Moves Toward Center Stage," *Wall Street Journal,* Dec. 11, 2009.

19. David Brooks, "The Pragmatic Leviathan," *New York Times,* Jan. 18, 2010; "Leviathan Stirs Again," *Economist,* Jan. 21, 2010; "The Whirlwind of Obama's Ambiguity," *RealClearPolitics.com,* Jan. 6, 2010. See also Richard Cohen, "Who Is Barack Obama?" *RealClearPolitics.com,* July 20, 2010.

20. Harold Meyerson, "Without a movement, progressives can't aid Obama's agenda," *Washington Post,* Jan. 6, 2010; Elizabeth Sanders, "Do-It-Yourself Governance: Without new social movements, there will be no new New Deal," *In These Times,* April 3, 2009; Michael Barone, "Getting Cold Feet Over Big Government," *RealClearPolitics.com,* July 9, 2009.

21. "The Obama Cult," *Economist,* July 25, 2009.

22. Gary Dean Best, *Pride, Prejudice, and Politics: Roosevelt versus Recovery, 1933–1938* (New York: Praeger Publishing, 1991), chap. 9; "U.S. Shifted Party, Not Ideology," *Wall Street Journal,* Jan. 19, 2010.

23. William Voegeli, "The Wilderness Years Begin," *Claremont Review of Books,* Spring 2009, 8–12; David Frum, "What the Tories Have to Teach Us," *Commentary,* November 2009, 36–38.

24. Kimberley Strassel, "The Right Ramps Up," *Wall Street Journal,* April 9, 2010; Joel Kotkin, "The Next Culture War," *Forbes.com,* July 28, 2009.

25. Stuart Rothenberg, "Are Dems Trying To Follow Past GOP Leaders Off the Cliff?" *RealClearPolitics.com,* Dec. 11, 2009; David Brooks, "A Moderate Manifesto," *New York Times,* March 2, 2009; Michael Gerson, "Liberal Agenda Struggling," *RealClearPolitics.com,* Sept. 11, 2009; Victor Davis Hanson, "Our Year of Obama," *National Review, Dec. 30, 2009.*

26. Dick Morris, *"The New Two-Party System," RealClearPolitics .com,* Jan. 6, 2010.

27. "Old Dogs and New Tricks," *Economist,* Feb. 11, 2010.

28. "Stop!" *Economist,* Jan. 23, 2010.

29. Arthur C. Brooks, "America's new culture war: Free enterprise vs. government control," *Washington Post,* May 23, 2010.

30. Daniel Henninger, "The Fall of the House of Kennedy," *Wall Street Journal,* Jan. 21, 2010; Peter Beinart, "Why Washington Is Tied Up in Knots," *Time,* Feb. 18, 2010; David Paul Kuhn, "The Enduring Mommy-Daddy Political Divide," *RealClearPolitics.com,* March 2, 2010; "Post poll question on smaller vs. larger government," *Washington Post,* April 28, 2010.

31. Gerson, "Liberal Agenda Struggling."

32. Jonah Goldberg, "Big Bedfellows," *National Review,* March 27, 2009; Julian Zelizer, "It's Obama's White House, but it's still Bush's world," *Washington Post,* Aug. 15, 2010.

CHAPTER FIVE

1. "Democrats Revive Immigration Push," *Wall Street Journal,* April 22, 2010.

2. William Voegeli, "Failed State," *Claremont Review of Books,* Fall 2009, 10–16.

3. "States Sink in Benefits Hole," *Wall Street Journal,* Feb. 18, 2010; "Fading are the peacemakers," *Economist,* Feb. 25, 2010. On California, Voegeli, "Failed State"; Steven Greenhut, "Class War," *Reason,* February 2010; on Ohio, James Nash, "Taxpayers asked to cover rising pension costs for government employees," *Columbus Dispatch,* Jan. 3, 2010; on Illinois, Amy Merrick, "Illinois Budget Woes Come to A Boil," *Wall Street Journal,* May 7, 2010. See also Mortimer Zuckerman, "The Bankrupting of America," *Wall Street Journal,* May 21, 2010; "Cash Crunch Will Force Governments to Do Less," *Wall Street Journal,* April 9, 2010; Megan McArdle, "Public Pensions Headed for Disaster," *Atlantic,* May 21, 2010.

4. "Payback Time: Padded Pensions Add to New York Fiscal Woes," *New York Times,* May 20, 2010.

5. "How Obama Came to Plan for 'Surge' in Afghanistan," *New York Times,* Dec. 5, 2009; Jonathan Alter, *The Promise: President Obama, Year One* (New York: Simon & Schuster, 2010), chap. 21.

6. "Timetable Reflects Isolationist Surge," *Wall Street Journal,* Dec. 4, 2008.

7. Walter Russell Mead, "The Carter Syndrome," *Foreign Policy,* January/February 2010; "Tough Enough?" *Economist,* May 30, 2009; "The Atlantic gap," *Economist,* Oct. 3, 2009.

8. Alan Dowd, "Declinism: Three centuries of gloomy forecasts about America," *Policy Review*, Aug. 1, 2007; Robert Kagan, "Neocon Nation: Neoconservatism, c. 1776," *World Affairs,* Spring 2008; Morton Keller, "Small Wars," *Philadelphia Inquirer,* Dec. 13, 2009. See also Walter Russell Mead, "Iran and Obama's Wilsonian Ideal," *RealClearPolitics .com,* July 10, 2010, on the possibility of Obama turning to a Wilsonian interventionism if Iran obtains a nuclear weapon.

9. "Reality Bites," *Economist,* Jan. 16, 2010.

10. "The visible hand," *Economist,* May 30, 2009.

11. Karl Rove, "The President Is No B + ," *Wall Street Journal,* Dec. 16, 2009.

12. Sidney Milkis and Jesse Rhodes, "Barack Obama, the Democratic Party, and the Future of the 'New American Party System,'" *The Forum* [online], vol. 7 (2009) no. 1.

13. David Brooks, "Liberal Suicide March," *New York Times,* July 20, 2009; Michael Barone, "When Liberal Leaders Confront a Centrist Nation," *RealClearPolitics.com,* Aug. 13, 2009; "Independents are calling the electoral shots," *Los Angeles Times,* Jan. 24, 2010.

14. For example, John Fund, "Tea Parties vs. Unions in November," *Wall Street Journal,* May 21, 2010.

15. Michael Barone, "Tuesday's Biggest Loser: The Union Agenda," *Wall Street Journal,* Nov. 4, 2009; "Republicans, riven but resurgent," *Economist,* Nov. 7, 2009; "Obama Trying to Turn Around His Presidency," *New York Times,* Jan. 20, 2010. See also "Voters Shifting to GOP, Poll Finds," *Wall Street Journal,* May 13, 2010.

16. "Obama's election year pitch leaves out white males," *Washington Examiner,* April 27, 2010; on LBJ, Sidney M. Milkis and Jerome M. Mileur, eds., *The Great Society and the High Tide of Liberalism* (Amherst, MA: University of Massachusetts Press, 2005), 35; Dick Morris, "The New Two-Party System," *RealClearPolitics.com,* Jan. 6, 2010; "Past may be prologue for congressional races," *Politico.com,* Nov. 10, 2009.

17. Michael Barone, "What 1946 Can Tell Us About 2010," *The American,* April 6, 2010; on LBJ, Michael Janeway, *The Fall of the House of Roosevelt* (New York: Columbia University Press, 2004), 194; on 1982, John B. Judis, "How to Stop the Bleeding," *New Republic,* March 15, 2010; "Clinton in '94 Gives Obama One Path to Follow in Defeat," *Wall Street Journal,* Jan. 22, 2010.

18. "Is it morning in America, or has hope given way to malaise?" *CNN.com*, Oct. 25, 2008.

19. "Where Clinton Turned Right, Obama Plowed Ahead," *New York Times*, Jan. 28, 2010; Douglas E. Schoen and Patrick H. Caddell, "How the Democrats can avoid a November bloodbath," *Washington Post*, April 16, 2010; John B. Judis, "Job One," *New Republic*, Sept. 22, 2009.

20. Jonah Goldberg, "Big Bedfellows," *National Review*, March 27, 2009; "The visible hand," *Economist*, May 30, 2009, 25.

21. John M. Blum, *Woodrow Wilson and the Politics of Morality* (Boston, Little, Brown, 1956); Robert Kagan, "Woodrow Wilson's Heir," *Washington Post*, June 7, 2009.

ABOUT THE AUTHOR

MORTON KELLER is the Spector Professor of History Emeritus at Brandeis University. He previously taught at the University of North Carolina and the University of Pennsylvania and has been a visiting professor at Harvard, Sussex, and Oxford, where he was the Harmsworth Professor of American History.

He is an elected member of the American Academy of Arts and Sciences and the British Academy. He has been a visiting scholar at the Hoover Institution since 2005.

His books include *The Life Insurance Enterprise, 1885–1910* (1963); *The Art and Politics of Thomas Nast* (1968); *Affairs of State: Public Life in Late Nineteenth Century America* (1977); *Regulating a New Economy* (1990); *Regulating a New Society* (1994); *Making Harvard Modern* (with Phyllis Keller) (2001); and *America's Three Regimes* (2007). His memoir, *My Times and Life: A Historian's Progress Through A Contentious Age*, is soon to be published by the Hoover Institution Press.

Articles by Keller have appeared in *Atlantic Monthly, Daedalus, The New Republic, The American Interest, The Wilson Quarterly,* and numerous scholarly journals.

INDEX